DEFENSE, SECURITY AND STRATEGIES

ACTS OF VIOLENCE IN THE FEDERAL WORKPLACE

PREVENTION AND RESPONSE GUIDE

DEFENSE, SECURITY AND STRATEGIES

Additional books in this series can be found on Nova's website under the Series tab.

Additional E-books in this series can be found on Nova's website under the E-book tab.

DEFENSE, SECURITY AND STRATEGIES

ACTS OF VIOLENCE IN THE FEDERAL WORKPLACE

PREVENTION AND RESPONSE GUIDE

FELIX TASH
EDITOR

nova publishers
New York

For permission to use material from this book please contact us:
Telephone 631-231-7269; Fax 631-231-8175
Web Site: http://www.novapublishers.com

Library of Congress Cataloging-in-Publication Data

ISBN: 978-1-62808-172-5

Published by Nova Science Publishers, Inc. † New York

CONTENTS

PREFACE

The protection of Federal employees and private citizens within U.S. government-owned or leased facilities is a top national priority. The mission of the Interagency Security Committee (ISC), comprised of 53 Federal departments and agencies, is to develop security standards, best practices, and guidelines for nonmilitary Federal facilities in the United States. This book provides important information to assist department and agency security planners as they address a growing issue becoming increasingly present throughout both the public and the private sector: acts of violence in the workplace. The book provides a variety of examples based on real-world events for planners to study and take into consideration.

Chapter 1 – According to the figures released by the Federal Bureau of Investigation (FBI), the estimated number of violent crimes in 2011 declined for the fifth consecutive year. The 2011 statistics show the estimated violent crime rate decreased 4.5% decrease from the 2010 rate. However and according to the latest known statistics from the Bureau of Labor Statistics (BLS), from 2006 to 2010, an average of 551 workers per year were killed as a result of work-related homicides. In 2010 (the last year for which final data are available), there was a reported total of 518 workplace homicides, or 11% of all fatal work injuries that occurred that year. Shootings accounted for 78% of all workplace homicides in 2010 (405 fatal injuries). More than four-fifths (83%) of these workplace homicides from shootings occurred in the private sector, while only 17% of such shootings occurred in government. Five percent of all establishments in the United States experienced a violent incident in 2005, and half of the largest establishments (employing 1,000 or more workers) reported at least one incident. No workplace is immune, and any government facility can serve as the setting for an incident of workplace violence. The April 1995 attack on the Alfred P. Murrah Federal Building in Oklahoma City provides an extreme example of how an office setting can be affected by workplace violence, in this case terrorism. This single act killed 168 people, injured 800 more, and was the largest terrorist attack on American soil prior to the September 11, 2001 attacks. It remains the most deadly terrorist attack ever perpetrated by an American citizen on American soil.

Fortunately, tragic events such as these are still the exception: most acts of workplace violence occur as some form of verbal or non-verbal threat, bullying, harassment, or non-fatal physical assault. However, it is important to remember acts of physical workplace violence might start as some form of nonphysical assault, so agencies must take all threats seriously and respond appropriately. It is also important to note a threat will not lead to a violent act in the great majority of cases. The threat itself, however, damages workplace safety and must be addressed.

Chapter 2 – The nature of criminal and terrorist threats to Federal facilities and employees has changed substantially over time, and it is management's job to ensure the effectiveness of protective measures changes as well. Employees want to know what the agency is doing to protect them and their facilities and what measures to take to protect themselves. Since it is impossible to know with any certainty whether a threat is going to be carried out, the agency should always approach facility and employee security in a serious manner and prepare as though a potential or known threat will evolve into a hostile act.

Physical security of nonmilitary Federal employees, contractors, visitors and facilities, has improved since the April 1995 attack on the Alfred P. Murrah Federal Building in Oklahoma City with the creation of the Interagency Security Committee (ISC). President Clinton issued Executive Order 12977 establishing the ISC that is today a component within the Department of Homeland Security. The ISC is a permanent body with representatives from over 50 Federal agencies and departments working together to address continuing government-wide security needs for Federal facilities. It establishes minimum security standards and oversees implementation of countermeasures to address current and future risks; thus, helping ensure the safety and security of nonmilitary Federal facilities and the individuals within them from all-hazards.

In: Acts of Violence in the Federal Workplace ISBN: 978-1-62808-172-5
Editor: Felix Tash

Chapter 1

VIOLENCE IN THE FEDERAL WORKPLACE: A GUIDE FOR PREVENTION AND RESPONSE[*]

Interagency Security Committee

MESSAGE FROM THE CHAIRPERSON

The protection of Federal employees and private citizens within U.S. government-owned or leased facilities is one of our top national priorities. The mission of the Interagency Security Committee (ISC), comprised of 53 Federal departments and agencies, is to develop security standards, best practices, and guidelines for nonmilitary Federal facilities in the United States.

[*] This is an edited, reformatted and augmented version of Interagency Security Committee, 1st Edition, dated April 2013.

As Chair of the ISC, I am pleased to introduce the new ISC guide titled *Violence in the Federal Workplace: A Guide for Prevention and Response*. This guide provides important information to assist department and agency security planners as they address a growing issue becoming increasingly present throughout both the public and the private sector: acts of violence in the workplace. To further assist Federal departments and agencies as they devise their plans, the guide provides planning suggestions to address and mitigate acts of violence in the Federal workplace. The guide also provides a variety of examples based on real-world events for planners to study and take into consideration.

This guide supersedes the Office of Personnel Management's handbook, *Dealing with Workplace Violence: A Guide for Agency Planners*, released in 1998. Consistent with Executive Order 12977 (October 19, 1995), this guide is intended to assist security planners for all buildings and facilities in the United States occupied by Federal employees for non-military activities. These include existing owned, to be purchased or leased facilities; stand-alone facilities; Federal campuses; and, where appropriate, individual facilities on Federal campuses and special-use facilities.

The guide contains significant updates and represents exemplary collaboration within the ISC working groups and across the entire ISC. ISC primary members approved the guide with full concurrence and will review and update as needed.

Caitlin Durkovich
Chair, Interagency Security Committee

EXECUTIVE SUMMARY

According to the figures released by the Federal Bureau of Investigation (FBI), the estimated number of violent crimes in 2011 declined for the fifth consecutive year. The 2011 statistics show the estimated violent crime rate decreased 4.5% decrease from the 2010 rate.[1] However and according to the latest known statistics from the Bureau of Labor Statistics (BLS), from 2006 to 2010, an average of 551 workers per year were killed as a result of work-related homicides. In 2010 (the last year for which final data are available), there was a reported total of 518 workplace homicides, or 11% of all fatal work injuries that occurred that year. Shootings accounted for 78% of all workplace homicides in 2010 (405 fatal injuries). More than four-fifths (83%)

of these workplace homicides from shootings occurred in the private sector, while only 17% of such shootings occurred in government.[2] Five percent of all establishments in the United States experienced a violent incident in 2005, and half of the largest establishments (employing 1,000 or more workers) reported at least one incident.[3] No workplace is immune, and any government facility can serve as the setting for an incident of workplace violence. The April 1995 attack on the Alfred P. Murrah Federal Building in Oklahoma City provides an extreme example of how an office setting can be affected by workplace violence, in this case terrorism. This single act killed 168 people, injured 800 more, and was the largest terrorist attack on American soil prior to the September 11, 2001 attacks. It remains the most deadly terrorist attack ever perpetrated by an American citizen on American soil.

Fortunately, tragic events such as these are still the exception: most acts of workplace violence occur as some form of verbal or non-verbal threat, bullying, harassment, or non-fatal physical assault. However, it is important to remember acts of physical workplace violence might start as some form of nonphysical assault, so agencies must take all threats seriously and respond appropriately. It is also important to note a threat will not lead to a violent act in the great majority of cases. The threat itself, however, damages workplace safety and must be addressed.

An act of workplace violence generally can be categorized as one of four types[4]:

- **Criminal Intent:** The perpetrator has no legitimate relationship to the agency or its employees and is usually committing a separate crime, such as robbery, in conjunction with the violence.
- **Customer/Client:** The perpetrator has a legitimate relationship with the agency and becomes violent while being served by the agency. This category includes customers, clients, patients, students, inmates, and any other group to whom the agency provides services. Employees working for government agencies servicing large segments of the public on a daily basis are likely to be exposed to this type of workplace violence.
- **Employee-on-Employee:** The perpetrator is a current or former agency employee who attacks or threatens another current or former employee(s) in the workplace.
- **Personal Relationship:** The perpetrator usually does not have a relationship with the agency but has a personal relationship with an

agency employee. This category includes domestic violence that spills over into the workplace.

It is also worth noting that, according to the Occupational Safety and Health Administration, workers are at greater risk of becoming victims of workplace violence if they:

- exchange money with the public;
- deliver passengers, goods, or services; or
- work alone or in small groups during late night or early morning hours,
- work in high-crime areas, or
- work in community settings and homes experiencing extensive contact with the public.[5]

In addition to the standard descriptions of incidents and the classification categories – mentioned above – in use since at least 2000, newer classification systems focus on triggers and intent, often distinguishing predatory from affective violence. Identifying triggers and intent supports risk assessment and prediction of recurrence and the required prevention strategies.[6]

ES.1. Planning, Prevention, and Response

Chapter 4 of the guide introduces a process for developing an effective workplace violence prevention and response program. It guides an agency's planning group through the basic steps of developing programs, policies, and prevention strategies.

ES.2. Investigations, Assessments, and Other

Chapter 5 offers basic technical information on several areas of expertise that may be involved in workplace violence programs at the individual level. Its purpose is to serve as a reference for planning group members as they find themselves working with colleagues whose professional backgrounds are different from their own. While in no way comprehensive enough to serve as a manual for training, it provides guidance to the planning group as it becomes more familiar with the larger issues entailed in the process of evaluating threat and determining a proper level of facility security. It also provides guidelines regarding the technical language, legal constraints, and special issues each person's professional background brings to the interdisciplinary group.

ES.3. Workplace Security

Violence in the Federal Workplace. A Guide for Prevention and Response, Appendix A. Threat Assessments, Countermeasures, Awareness, and Case Studies (hereafter referred to as Appendix A) provides general information regarding the process of evaluating threat to Federal facilities and making a Facility Security Level determination, two critically important pieces of any program aimed at preventing and responding to violence in the Federal workplace. Appendix A starts with a brief introduction to the risk assessment and management processes facilities' management should implement and maintain for the physical security of nonmilitary Federal facilities. Such attention to the physical security of a facility can enhance the degree of deterrence against an act of workplace violence as well as the degree of mitigation should an act of violence occur.

ES.4. Awareness and Resources

Also listed in Appendix A are Federal government, non-Federal government, and computer system resources either used to develop this guide or available to the reader for further research and information. A listing of the Department of Homeland Security's free courses, materials, and workshops to better prepare the public to deal with an active shooter situations and to raise awareness of behaviors that represent pre-incident indicators and characteristics of active shooters can also be found in this section.

The information provided in this guide is based on the collective expertise and experience of Federal Government law enforcement officers, security specialists, criminal investigators, attorneys, employee relations specialists, Employee assistance program counselors, forensic psychologists, and union officials. It consists primarily of "lessons learned" from many years of experience with actual cases involving potentially violent employees. The guidance covers not only the macro issues of facility security, but also incidents of physical violence such as shootings and assaults and the far more prevalent incidents of intimidation, "bullying," and other inappropriate behaviors. It also covers incidents involving employees and incidents involving individuals from outside the agency threatening violence against agency employees.

ES.5. Case Studies

The last section in Appendix A presents case studies for the planning group to use in analyzing agency needs, planning programs, and training personnel to respond to instances of workplace violence. The case studies introduce a wide range of challenges an agency may face and provide discussion questions to help the planning group develop the most effective approaches to these challenges.

1.0. Introduction

This document supersedes and updates the handbook produced by the U.S. Office of Personnel Management (OPM) in 1998 and includes updates contributed by the Interagency Security Committee Working Group on Violence in the Federal Workplace. It provides both a framework for Federal departments and agencies to use in the protection of the Federal workforce and facilities from acts of violence as well as guidelines for creating workplace violence prevention and response programs. The document also addresses facility security issues unique to such incidents.

Workplace violence can potentially affect every Federal employee throughout the United States. It is the responsibility of Federal managers and supervisors to plan for a wide variety of potential incidents that could impact their employees and facilities. The continuum of violent acts ranges from the more common non-physical acts such as incivility, bullying, gestures, expressions, and verbal threats to the less common physical acts such as battery, aggravated assault, homicide, and acts of terrorism. Violence or threats of violence can occur anywhere. For the purpose of this document, the workplace includes numerous types of environments such as, but not limited to, office space, retail settings, and field work.

Any Federal worker, including office workers with little public contact, can be exposed to workplace violence. Acts of violence in the workplace generally fall into one of four categories:

1) Criminal intent;
2) Customer/client;
3) Employee on employee; or
4) Personal relationship.

As part of a comprehensive workplace hazard prevention and response program, it starts with management commitment and employee involvement. Equally important is the understanding that, while human resource components may serve as the lead in development of the program, different scenarios may require different offices/personnel to serve as the primary lead for the response when an act of violence occurs. However, the program's ultimate success depends on teamwork both within and outside the organization. As such, it is important to involve the recognized labor organizations in the workplace in the early stages of program development. As employee representatives and advocates, labor organizations can provide valuable input on programs affecting the health and safety of the Federal workforce. Planning team members should include, for example, facility security staff and local and state law enforcement and emergency personnel when developing actual plans and programs (discussed in Chapter 4).

Victims and coworkers who survive workplace assaults may experience psychological distress or physical injury. Federal employees in organizations such as the National Institute for Occupational Safety and Health (NIOSH) and the Occupational Safety and Health Administration (OSHA) play a leading role in helping employers recognize and respond appropriately to the risks and consequences of workplace violence. At the same time, the risk of violence specifically directed against Federal employees received increased attention over time, particularly in the wake of the tragic loss of life in the terrorist bombing of the Alfred P. Murrah Federal Building in Oklahoma City on April 19, 1995.

Even before the Oklahoma City tragedy, Federal managers and specialists, like their private sector counterparts, were becoming more aware of the dangers of workplace violence and began developing preventive programs for their employees. This was a challenging endeavor. When they turned to the private sector for expert guidance, they often found the advice either was not necessarily compatible with Federal laws and regulations or failed to cover issues faced by Federal employees. However, in attempting to develop their own programs, agencies often discovered they lacked the expertise necessary for a truly comprehensive approach.

To complicate matters further for program planners (both then and now), public interest and media attention tend to focus on dramatic but rare incidents of violence, such as shootings in office settings. This presents the dual challenge of reducing employees' anxiety about rare risk factors while focusing their attention on more likely sources of danger. Undue anxiety about relatively infrequent but high profile incidents can stand in the way of identifying more significant but less dramatic risk factors such as poorly lit parking lots or gaps in employee training programs. This anxiety can make it more difficult to cope with one of the most common workplace violence problems: the employee whose language or behavior frightens coworkers.

2.0. PURPOSE

The Occupational Safety and Health Act of 1970[7] (the Act) was written, "...to assure safe and healthful working conditions for working men and women ...." Among its specifications, it stipulated:

- The development and promulgation of occupational safety and health standards by the Department of Labor (Section 6 of the Act, 29 USC §655) that led to the creation of OSHA. OSHA is tasked with, among other things, developing, promulgating, and enforcing the standards required by Section 6 of the Act.
- The requirement for Federal agencies to establish and maintain occupational safety and health programs (Section 19 of the Act, 29 USC §668) that led to the development of Executive Order (EO) 12196, Occupational Safety and Health Programs for Federal Employees, issued February 26, 1980. EO 12196 prescribes additional responsibilities for the heads of Federal agencies, the Secretary of Labor, and the General Services Administration (GSA). Among other things, the Secretary of Labor, through OSHA, is required to issue basic program elements for Federal agency occupational safety and health (OSH) programs. These basic program elements are set forth in 29 CFR §1960.
- The creation of the National Institute of Occupational Safety and Health (NIOSH) as part of the Centers for Disease Control and

Prevention in the Department of Health and Human Services (Section 22 of the Act, 29 USC §671) that performs research in fields related to occupational safety and health, and provides OSH-related information, education, and training. NIOSH is a world leader in helping to prevent work-related illness, injury, disability, and death through its activities of gathering information, conducting scientific research, and translating the resulting knowledge gained into a variety of products and services, such as training materials and recommendations for improving safety and health in the workplace.

Section 19 of the Act, EO 12196, and the basic program elements under 29 CFR §1960 apply to all agencies of the Executive Branch except military personnel and uniquely military equipment, systems, and operations. Within OSHA, the Office of Federal Agency Programs provides Federal agencies with the guidance necessary to implement effective occupational safety and health programs.

While OSHA did not promulgate a regulation specific to workplace violence, 29 CFR §1960.8(a) requires agencies to "furnish to each employee employment and a place of employment which are free from recognized hazards that are causing or are likely to cause death or serious physical harm." Much like Section 5(a)(1) of the Act is the "General Duty Clause" for private sector employers, this regulation tasks Executive Branch agencies with the general duty of protecting Federal employees from workplace hazards not covered by specific OSHA standards.

EO 12977 established the Interagency Security Committee (ISC) pursuant to the recommendations contained in the Department of Justice's *Vulnerability Assessment of Federal Facilities*[8] report issued in June 1995. The ISC's mandate is to establish security policies and standards "to enhance the quality and effectiveness of security in and protection of buildings and facilities in the United States occupied by federal employees for nonmilitary activities ...."

3.0. CONTRIBUTORS

The ISC recognizes the Federal partners who provided resources and staff time for preparation of this document. These partners include: the Department of Health and Human Services' (HHS) Office of Security and Strategic Information, OSHA's ISC Chief Human Capital Officers Council,

Department of Labor, Department of Homeland Security's (DHS) Federal Protective Service (FPS), OPM, United States Postal Service, United States Postal Inspection Service, Department of Commerce, Department of Defense's Defense Information Systems Agency; Department of Veterans Affairs' Veterans Health Administration (VHA), and Uniform Services University of the Health Sciences.

This guide builds upon the contributions of experts from many professions and many Federal agencies. The ISC wishes to thank OPM and everyone who contributed to the development of the OPM handbook *Dealing with Workplace Violence: A Guide for Agency Planners* (1998), particularly the work conducted by the Department of Justice and FPS on issues concerning law enforcement and security. Special thanks also go to those individuals who lent their expertise, experience, and talents to OPM's effort in providing answers to some of the more difficult questions about handling potentially violent situations. For a list of individual contributors to *Violence in the Federal Workplace: A Guide for Prevention and Response*, please see Appendix A.

4.0. Planning, Prevention and Response

The central theme emerging from the shared experience of these specialists from different disciplines is this: while some cases of workplace violence can be dealt with swiftly and easily by a supervisor with the assistance of just one specialist or one office, most cases can be resolved more easily and effectively if there is a joint effort planned in advance by specialists from different disciplines.

Many people who have never experienced workplace violence believe it will never happen in their office. Violent incidents are relatively rare, but they do occur and lives can be lost. A little preparation and investment in prevention could save a life. There is no strategy that works for every situation, yet the likelihood of a successful resolution is much greater if there are preparations.

In dealing with the more common incidents generated by employees, the experience of agencies with developed programs show supervisors are more willing to confront employees who exhibit disruptive and intimidating behavior when they are supported by a group of trained and experienced specialists. Supervisors who receive training are prepared to reach out to others when they know a situation is beyond their expertise. This team approach promotes creative solutions and much needed support for the supervisors in dealing with difficult situations that might otherwise be ignored.

Ignoring a situation usually results in escalation of the problem. Morale and productivity are lowered and effective employees leave the organization. On the other hand, dealing effectively with situations like hostility, intimidation, and disruptive conflict creates a more productive workplace. This can have a deterrent effect on anyone contemplating or prone to committing acts of physical violence. Employees will see improper actions have consequences and disruptive behavior is not tolerated in their organization.

4.1. Section 1: Program Development

Workplace violence can occur in any work environment. For this reason, it is important for all Federal agencies to establish a written workplace violence prevention program. Successful workplace violence prevention strategies are multi-dimensional, encompassing a structured training program as well as clearly established reporting and incident communication procedures. Training ensures workers are aware of potential hazards and how to respond when a violent situation occurs. Employees should be encouraged to report incidents with the assurance management will take such reports seriously and act on them promptly and appropriately. Finally, the agency's communication procedures should be defined for all levels and employees should receive training on communication strategies and techniques.

There are many different approaches agencies can take in developing plans to prevent workplace violence. An approach that works well in one agency may not be suitable for another. This section outlines some broad guidelines to assist agencies:

- Analyze their current ability to handle potentially violent situations;
- Fill any existing skill gaps;
- Develop a procedure for employees to report incidents; and
- Develop response plans.

4.1.1. Forming a Planning Group

Successful agency programs usually start by forming a planning group. The planning group evaluates the agency's current ability to handle violent incidents and recommends ways to strengthen its response capability.

Typically, members of a planning group include representatives from management, employee relations, employee assistance program (EAP), law enforcement, and security. Organizations too small to have a law enforcement/security component often have a representative of FPS (when they have jurisdiction) or the local police. Depending on the size and structure of the agency, membership may also include representatives from safety, health unit, medical department, office of Equal Employment Opportunity, public affairs, and other appropriate offices. The planning group should identify a lead member with primary responsibility for developing and implementing the organization's workplace violence prevention and response policy and programs.

The Office of the General Counsel (OGC) and the Office of Inspector General (OIG) should always be extended an invitation to participate in the planning group. When these offices are not represented on the planning group, they usually act as consultants to it.

While many offices may be represented on the planning group, only a few of them will generally be involved in responding to reported incidents. For example, representatives from employee relations, EAP, and security often make up the incident response team. Typically, representatives from the other offices will not be involved in responding directly to incidents, but they will act as consultants to the incident response team and play an active role only in certain types of situations. In addition, to better coordinate and maximize the effectiveness of prevention and response efforts, co-located agencies should have one unified response plan in place rather than each agency creating a separate plan.

4.1.2. Working with Your Union

An agency should involve the recognized facility labor union(s) early in the process of planning workplace violence prevention and response programs. Unions are the elected representatives of bargaining unit employees and are legally entitled to negotiate over many conditions of employment of those employees. Although some of the substantive issues relating to workplace violence, including issues concerning internal security may be outside the duty to bargain, this does not negate consultation and discussion with the union.

Union involvement is particularly appropriate where there are labor management partnership councils. It is a good practice to involve recognized unions before policy decisions are made to provide them the opportunity both to express employees' concerns and to bring to bear their expertise and knowledge.

4.1.3. Steps in the Planning Process

1. Analyze Agency's Current Ability to Handle Potentially Violent Situations

Conducting a risk assessment and analysis of the agency's current ability to handle potentially violent situations is the first step in the planning process. Looking at previous incidents that occurred at the agency and in the area and evaluating the causes and how effectively they were handled is a good way to start. Attention should be given to identifying patterns of risk and potential prevention strategies; for example, where a particular workgroup is having a number of complaints in a given period of time.

Also, reviewing the case studies in Appendix A of this guide and analyzing the incident response of other agencies can help planning groups determine if their own agency is prepared to handle similar occurrences.

Staff Expertise

Managers should be aware of specialized organizations within their agencies and the policies relating to their defined roles and responsibilities. Identifying and understanding the agency's in-house capabilities enables them to lead an effort incorporating staff expertise into the organization's program, whether in the area of prevention or in designing an appropriate response. Identifying gaps in specific skills, such as threat assessment and management, may guide training plans.

Level of Security and Jurisdictional Issues

An important part of the analysis is to examine the current level of security of the facility. Follow the advice of the security office or, if in a building without a security staff, contact FPS (when they have jurisdiction), the agency's internal police force if available, or local law enforcement about recommended basic security measures. Determine in advance all jurisdictional issues among the various security and law enforcement entities that may be involved in an emergency situation.

Response time is one of the critical factors in addressing incidents of workplace violence. All employees should be informed as to the security and/or law enforcement entities they should contact in the event of an incident. Contact information for those security and/or law enforcement entities should be made available to all employees.

2. Fill The Skill Gaps

Skill deficiencies exist even in large agencies with numerous resources at hand. In some organizations training is needed (see Chapter 4, Section 3 for a discussion of training). However, crisis situations occur infrequently, and it is often not practical to maintain in-house expertise for every aspect of the agency's response plan.

If this is the case, suggested sources of outside assistance are listed below.

Other Government Agencies

Get to know specialists in other government agencies. Federal agencies often share expertise, especially when crisis situations occur. They are also an invaluable source for learning about new training materials and effective training approaches.

Law Enforcement Agencies

If either in-house law enforcement or FPS is available, get to know the responders. Keep in mind many personnel who are not in the security arena or are not accustomed to working with police personnel may find interaction somewhat intimidating. Invite the responders to an informal meeting that allows for positive dialogue and an opportunity for non-security personnel to ask questions and get to know the responders. In addition, add them to the planning group. In-house law enforcement and the FPS can provide valuable insight as to how they will respond and assist your group.

In the event in-house law enforcement or FPS is not available, get to know local law enforcement officers. Invite them to work with the planning group. They can recommend security measures, and identify jurisdiction, and what they would do if called during an incident. They can also teach employees personal safety techniques on how to avoid becoming a victim.

Other Community Resources

Locate and work with resources in the community. For example, if there is no immediate access to emergency mental health consultation, work with the local community mental health department, "hotline" staff, hospital, or emergency crisis center. A nearby university may have faculty who are willing to be consulted.

3. Develop a Procedure for Employees to Report Incidents

The primary consideration in developing a reporting procedure in the context of a workplace violence program is to make sure it encourages employees to report all incidents, even minor ones. Employees should report all incidents to management if he or she is the victim of violence, believes he or she has been threatened with violence, witnesses an act or threat of violence towards anyone else, or has reason to believe he, she, or others may be victimized sometime in the future at the workplace or as a result of employment with the agency. Generally the agency's Occupant Emergency Plan (OEP) or other emergency plan has established reporting mechanisms. Planners should review those procedures to determine whether, for purposes of workplace violence incidents, any specialized procedures are appropriate. Credibility for any reporting system will be dependent upon whether reports are quickly, effectively, and confidentiality handled.

Before a reporting procedure is announced to employees, ensure the agency staff who will be responding to reported incidents are trained and able to handle any reported incidents.

Also important to the success of any reporting system is management's encouragement for reporting incidents. Agency managers must create an environment demonstrating management will always respond immediately to reports of incidents and to employee concerns in order to protect employees from danger, unnecessary anxiety concerning their welfare, and the loss of productivity.

Incident reports should be reviewed on a periodic basis to provide feedback for lessons learned.

4. Develop Plans to Respond to Workplace Violence Incidents

Given the wide range of incidents and situations that can occur at the worksite (from disruptive behavior to shootings) and, within that range, the wide variation of threatening and disruptive behaviors, it is difficult for agencies to specifically define the responsibilities of the different offices possibly involved in responding to an incident under a workplace violence prevention and response program. Agencies found it useful to classify incidents in broad categories such as emergency/non-emergency, emergency/threats/bullying/disruptive behavior, or coworker/outsider. Some agencies belong to industry groups with predictable risks, such as health care, corrections, and education, as the vast majority of violence incidents in the workplace arise from client-professional interactions. Those may require formal standing approaches to threat assessment and management.

One such example is the Disruptive Behavior Committee and Patient Record Flagging process in health care developed in the Veterans Health Administration (VHA). Such interdisciplinary committees are standing groups trained to assess incidents, evaluate the risk of recurrence, and provide guidance on prevention in the future. Training addresses clinical threat assessment and law enforcement issues. Employee threat assessment teams function under a different set of rules, such as patient care delivery, and in a clinical system and has different rules than human resources regulations under OPM. Corrections facilities have other obvious regulatory constraints and opportunities, and those influence fundamental strategies in threat assessment and management. Agencies must consider their administrative rules and processes in order to remain within the appropriate boundaries before such incidents occur.

> It is unlawful to possess firearms or other dangerous weapons in Federal facilities, unless explicitly authorized by 18 USC §930. Federal agencies must post the notice in the Appendix to § 102-72 of the Code of Federal Regulations. Agency employees should be trained to report suspected violations immediately to a building security official, a supervisor, or other appropriate authority.

Using these broad categories, agencies can determine the offices that would generally respond to each type of incident and what role each office would play in the response effort. Agencies can appropriately plan for both immediate responses and long-term responses.

To facilitate developing a plan that works for a given agency, a series of case studies are provided in Appendix A of this guide providing examples of the plans used to handle a number of situations.

It becomes apparent from reviewing these examples that plans for a coordinated response to reported incidents must be kept flexible. Responsibility for overall coordination and direction is usually assigned to one individual or one office. The coordinator must have the flexibility to use the plan as a guideline and not a mandatory set of procedures. More importantly, the coordinator must have the latitude to tailor the recommended response to the particular situation. It is important to recognize threatening situations often require creative responses. Given this, the importance of flexibility cannot be overemphasized.

Violence cannot always be prevented because violent incidents are not always predictable, but risk can be reduced by planning ahead and being prepared to act swiftly to deal with threats, intimidation, and other disruptive behavior at an early stage.

The case studies in Appendix A highlight the need for backup plans in situations calling for an immediate response where the individual responsible for a certain aspect of the response effort is unavailable. Taking a team approach in responding to a potentially violent situation is an ideal way to provide backup coverage. A team approach ensures all staff in employee relations, EAP, security, and other offices are thoroughly trained and prepared to work together with management to deal with potentially violent situations. It ensures coverage regardless of which staff member in each of the offices is on duty when an incident occurs.

4.2. Section 2: Development of Written Policy Statements

4.2.1. Advantages of Written Policies

Once a workplace violence prevention and response program is ready to be implemented, agencies must decide whether to issue a written policy statement. There are advantages to issuing a statement. It informs employees the violence policy covers intimidation, harassment, and other inappropriate behavior that threatens or frightens them. It also encourages employees to report incidents, informs employees of how to report an incident, and demonstrates senior management's commitment to dealing with reported incidents.

Agency programs can also be implemented without a written policy statement. In agencies without a written policy statement, employees are often given information about the program (especially how to report an incident) in training sessions, on posters, in newsletter articles, or by other similar methods. It is important to note agencies have an inherent right to take action against employees who engage in disruptive or threatening behavior regardless if the agency issued a written policy statement or not.

4.2.2. Policy Statement Contents

A workplace violence policy statement should convey that:

- All employees are responsible for maintaining a safe work environment;
- Employees are obligated to act appropriately on the job;
- The policy covers not only acts of physical violence, but also harassment, intimidation,
- and other disruptive behavior;

- The policy covers incidents involving coworkers and incidents involving individuals
- from outside the agency who commit violence against agency employees;
- The agency will respond appropriately to all reported incidents; and
- The agency will act to stop inappropriate behavior.

Supervisors and all of the offices involved in responding to incidents will be supported by agency management, in accordance with their individual agency's plans, in their efforts to deal with violent and potentially violent situations. The policy statement should also provide examples clearly indicating some of the behaviors that constitute workplace violence, along with specifying prohibited actions and their consequences. Examples of prohibited behaviors could include but are not limited to:

- Direct threats or physical intimidation;
- Implications or suggestions of violence;
- Stalking;
- Possession of weapons of any kind on agency property, including parking lots, other
- exterior agency premises, or while engaged in agency activities in other locations or at
- agency-sponsored events, unless such possession or use is a requirement of the job;
- Assault of any form;
- Physical restraint or confinement;
- Dangerous or threatening horseplay;
- Loud, disruptive, or angry behavior or language that is clearly not part of the typical work
- environment;
- Blatant or intentional disregard for the safety or well-being of others; Commission of a violent felony or misdemeanor on agency property; and
- Any act that a reasonable person would perceive as constituting a threat of violence.

4.2.3. Recommended Approaches

Consider the following recommendations in developing a written policy statement.

A written policy statement should be brief and simple. Implementation details can be provided in training and in more detailed backup documents. For example, roles and responsibilities of the various offices involved in responding to potentially dangerous situations can be outlined in memoranda of understanding or in operating manuals/instructions rather than in the written policy statement issued to all agency employees. This approach gives agency staff the flexibility they will need to deal creatively with fluid, unpredictable situations.

There are disadvantages to using defined terms such as violence, threats, and harassment in your written policy statement. Definitions can discourage employees from reporting incidents they do not believe fall within the definition. The reporting system should not deter employees from reporting situations they feel are of a threatening nature. An employee knows a threat or intimidation or other disruptive behavior when he or she experiences it; definitions are not necessary. The scope of the organization's concept of one or more of the terms in the policy can be clarified by use of examples. For instance, you may want to give examples of verbal and nonverbal intimidating behavior.

Another consideration is that definitions are often restrictive and may create legal problems in the future when taking disciplinary actions against perpetrators of workplace violence. Use of definitions can make it more difficult to defend a case on appeal. For example, there could be negative consequences from employing the term "zero tolerance." Use of the term could make it more difficult to defend a case on appeal because a third party could conclude, however mistaken and inappropriate, the agency did not consider an appropriate penalty for the particular offense. There are other possible consequences. The term "zero tolerance" might appear to eliminate any flexibility an agency has in dealing with difficult situations even if there is a lack of intent on the part of the perpetrator. Another undesirable side effect is the appearance of inflexibility can discourage employees from reporting incidents because they do not want to get their co-worker fired when they just want the behavior stopped. This appearance of inflexibility may also discourage early intervention in potentially violent situations.

Consult OGC for the legal implications of the draft policy. Agencies wishing to issue a written policy statement can use the following sample, changing the format and tone as appropriate, and adapting it for their own situations. The following sample written policy statement contains language similar to "zero tolerance" but addresses the previously mentioned concerns. It says the agency will not tolerate violent or disruptive behavior and then clarifies what that means by stating "that is, all reports of incidents will be taken seriously and dealt with appropriately."

> MEMORANDUM FOR EMPLOYEES
> OF THE DEPARTMENT OF ______________
> FROM: DEPARTMENT OR AGENCY HEAD
> SUBJECT: Workplace Violence
>
> It is the [insert Department or Agency name]'s policy to promote a safe environment for its employees. The Department is committed to working with its employees to maintain a work environment free from incidents that could be construed as violence, threats of violence, harassment, intimidation, and other disruptive behavior. While this kind of conduct is not pervasive at our agency, no agency is immune. Every agency will be affected by disruptive behavior at one time or another.
>
> Violence, threats, harassment, intimidation, and other disruptive behavior in our workplace will not be tolerated; that is, all reports of incidents will be taken seriously and will be dealt with appropriately. Such behavior can include oral or written statements, gestures, or expressions that communicate a direct or indirect threat of physical harm. Individuals who commit such acts may be removed from the premises and may be subject to disciplinary action, criminal penalties, or both.
>
> Your cooperation is critical to implementing this policy effectively and maintaining a safe working environment. Do not ignore violent, threatening, harassing, intimidating, or other disruptive behavior. If you observe or experience such behavior by anyone on agency premises, whether he or she is an agency employee or not, report it immediately to a supervisor or manager. Supervisors and managers who receive such reports should seek advice from the Employee Relations Office at xxx-xxx-xxxx regarding investigating the incident and initiating appropriate action. [**PLEASE NOTE**: Threats or assaults that require immediate attention by security or police should be reported first to security at xxx-xxx-xxxx or to police at 911.]
>
> I will support all efforts made by supervisors and agency specialists in dealing with violent, threatening, harassing, intimidating, or other disruptive behavior in our workplace and will monitor whether this policy is being implemented effectively. If you have any questions about this policy statement, please contact __________ at xxx-xxx-xxxx.

Figure 1. Sample Written Policy Statement.

4.3. Section 3: Prevention

One major component of any workplace violence program is prevention. The topics in the previous sections, such as program development and union involvement, are important parts of a workplace violence prevention program. This section will focus on additional measures that can be taken to reduce the risk of violent behavior.

4.3.1. Workplace Violence Prevention Program

All workplace violence prevention programs should meet minimum requirements set forth in Section 19 of the Act, EO 12196, and the basic program elements under 29 CFR § 1960. In addition, it is important to conduct an annual audit of the program to determine any changes that need to be addressed. A sample workplace violence prevention program checklist is provided at the end of this section for reference.

4.3.1.1. Facility Security and Protection

Agencies should use their existing OEPs as the starting point when developing a workplace violence prevention program. The plan should include where applicable and not limited to:

- Notification protocols for reporting incidents;
- Plan initiation and communication;
- Employee notification, communication, and instructions;
- Procedures for determining whether to evacuate, shelter-in-place, or deep shelter a
- facility;
- Contingency plans for maintaining facility operations;
- Establishment of threat assessment teams (employee and client);
- Chain of command and notification protocols;
- Perimeter security/deep shelter if applicable;
- Protective force communication/protocols;
- Protective force equipment donning guidelines;
- Plans for conducting training exercises, drills, and other response and preparedness
- evaluations;
- Initial responder notification protocols;
- Incident command hierarchy and instructions;
- Medical response and resource; and

- Coordination and response planning with other compound facilities such as adjacent day-
- care facilities or other neighboring entities.

4.3.1.2. Reporting

Accurate and early reporting that provides for a well-timed intervention can be instrumental in resolving issues of workplace incivility and bullying before incidents escalate into physical violence. Developing and implementing reporting procedures for workplace bullying and incivility are just as important as establishing procedures for reporting physical violence.

Employees who feel they are victims of bullying, verbal or electronic harassment/cyber bullying (e.g. e-mails, text messages, web-pages), psychological violence, or emotional abuse need to report the problem as these behaviors can negatively impact the victim, work environment, and employee productivity. Employees may want to document the incidents in order to assist with remembering the details, dates, and frequency of the incidents. Early reporting of perceived abuse allows management to quickly address and correct a problem before it has the opportunity to become more severe. The level of the management chain where an employee reports this type of incident will depend on who is committing the non-physical violence. If a direct supervisor is the perpetrator, then the employee needs to move up one level on the management chain to report the violence.

Procedures for reporting workplace violence incidents vary according to the type and intensity of violence involved, and most Federal workplaces have a variety of reporting options. Depending on the nature of the situation, resources available in-house, and the need for security/law enforcement involvement, the report may go to one or more of the following:

- The employee's supervisor;
- In-house security;
- Threat assessment team;
- FPS; or
- Local law enforcement.

In addition to established reporting procedures, agencies should allow for employees who have safety or reprisal concerns to submit anonymous (to the extent possible) reports. Regardless of the specific reporting procedures, maintaining a successful workplace violence prevention and response program requires agencies to investigate all reports and follow up with the appropriate actions where necessary. However, agencies should keep in mind that if there is no complainant, a law enforcement entity may feel there is no crime to investigate.

4.3.1.3. Communication

Prompt, accurate communication during a workplace violence incident or any other type of emergent event is essential. The communication section of the workplace violence plan should identify how the agency will notify the affected employees and facility occupants and who will provide that notification. Also, this section of the plan must include provisions for communicating information to employees who have a vision or hearing impairment and/or for those whom English is not their primary language.

4.3.1.4. Field Worker Concerns

Special measures need to be implemented for workers assigned to field locations or who perform their duties outside a Federal facility. Circumstances related to field work present a different set of concerns for workplace violence incidents. Workers have encountered violence while conducting compliance inspections, home visits, customer service duties, and other field assignments.

Each field assignment involves its own set of risk factors for violence. It is essential employees on assignment in the field be trained and provided with assignment-specific safety guidelines. Other techniques useful for increasing the safety of field assignments and working environments include but are not limited to:

- A communication system including a designated contact at the home office;
- A daily work plan, schedule, and predetermined phone call check-in times;
- A “buddy system” (i.e. a partner); and/or
- Law enforcement back-up.

4.3.1.5. Workplace Violence Incident Response

Regardless of the nature of the workplace violence incident, the safety and security of all employees must be a top priority for any response personnel. It is important to understand workplace violence incidents do not necessarily get reported via a phone call to security. The security response process must be flexible enough to handle any situation that manifests in the workplace and in whatever manner it may be reported. While Federal agencies already have a variety of emergency response-oriented plans, the workplace violence response plan must also consider the threat may arise internally rather than externally.

4.3.1.6. Facility Response

A threat of workplace violence, whether external or internal, may result in the need to evacuate the facility, shelter-in-place, or enact a deep shelter status. The facility's OEP should address what action is appropriate for the situation.

- If evacuation of the facility is necessary, then following the emergency evacuation plan procedures will result in a prompt and orderly evacuation of occupants in a quick and safe manner.
- In an instance where the threatening situation is occurring from the exterior or perimeter of the facility, sheltering-in-place may be the safest course of action. This shelter-in-place area should be pre-designated internal location that has been chosen to protect individuals when conditions outside the facility are more dangerous than inside or when outside conditions are unknown.
- Some types of workplace violence events may result in a deep shelter mode being ordered. During a "deep shelter" employees will be told to stay in their current locations, lock doors and other access points, and refrain from moving to other locations within the facility until the threat has been mitigated.

To ensure employees are prepared for potential evacuation, the agency should distribute to each employee a viable occupant emergency plan outlining procedures to follow in the event of fire, bomb threats, civil demonstrations, threats of violence both inside and outside the office, natural disasters, etc.

4.3.1.7. Domestic Violence in the Workplace

Every instance of domestic violence that spills into the workplace is different; it is likely that separate action plans will be necessary for each individual's situation. Domestic violence can occur in the workplace in the form of harassing or threatening phone calls or emails to the victim, visits to the workplace, increased employee absenteeism, and other personal or electronic harassment/intimidation tactics.

The perpetrator usually has an indirect connection to the workplace through a current or previous relationship with an employee. The offender may be an employee's current or former spouse or significant other, a relative, or a friend.

Victims can change their contact information and residences, but most are reluctant to do so and have some level of difficulty in changing jobs. Perpetrators of domestic violence use this fact to their advantage to gain access to the victims. A victim of domestic violence should inform their employer so their employer can take steps to prevent the violence from extending into the workplace. Some strategies that may be helpful include:

- Providing copies of restraining orders (if any) and a recent photo to security and management to prevent the perpetrator from entering the facility;
- Providing flexible scheduling;
- Offering security escorts to and from parking areas;
- Ensuring the employee is aware of employee assistance programs;
- Offering the employee use of a buddy system;
- Offering the employee transfer to another job; and/or
- Relocating the job and employee to another facility.

4.3.2. Warning Signs of Violence

The first question many people ask when starting to develop a workplace violence prevention and response program is: How can we identify potentially violent individuals? It is understandable that people want to know, and that "early warning signs" and "profiles" of potentially violent employees are in much of the literature on the subject of workplace violence. It would save time and solve problems if supervisors could recognize ahead of time what behaviors and personality traits are predictive of future violent actions.

4.3.2.1. Indicators of Potentially Violent Behavior

No one can accurately predict violent behavior in non-mental health, non-institutionalized populations. However, indicators of increased risk of violent behavior are available. These indicators have been identified by the Federal Bureau of Investigation (FBI) National Center for the Analysis of Violent Crime, Profiling and Behavioral Assessment Unit in its analysis of past incidents of workplace violence.[9] These are some of the indicators:

- Direct or veiled threats of harm;
- Intimidating, belligerent, harassing, bullying, or other inappropriate and aggressive behavior;

- Numerous conflicts with supervisors and other employees;
- Bringing a weapon to the workplace, brandishing a weapon in the workplace, making inappropriate references to guns, or fascination with weapons;
- Statements showing fascination with incidents of workplace violence, statements indicating approval of the use of violence to resolve a problem, or statements indicating identification with perpetrators of workplace homicides;
- Statements indicating desperation (over family, financial, and other personal problems) to the point of contemplating suicide;
- Pending or recent layoffs;
- Drug/alcohol abuse; and
- Extreme changes in behavior.

Each of these behaviors is a clear sign that something is wrong. None of these signs should be ignored. By identifying the problem and dealing with it appropriately, supervisors may be able to prevent violence from happening.

One cannot tally the factors, arrive at a “score,” and then render from that score a probability violence will occur. Because each violence risk factor is embedded in a unique context, a given factor may contribute to the risk formulation to varying degrees. The subject who exhibits only one of the factors listed may in fact pose an extreme risk of violence if that one factor is something like "brandishing a weapon in the hospital workplace while staring intently at her doctor."

A thorough threat assessment will also consider any "good news" in relation to the subject. That means mitigating factors against the risk of violence must also be considered. For example, a disruptive employee with a strong desire and commitment to complete his/her Federal career and retire may present less actual risk of further violence than another employee who has no expectation of reaching retirement. A subject with strong family connections and no wish to disappoint others similarly may pose less of a risk. Sometimes strong religious conviction will mitigate violence. These and other possible mitigating factors should be evaluated as part of a complete threat assessment while maintaining the subject’s privacy.

Agency planning groups should ensure the appropriate staff member (or an incident response team) is prepared to assist supervisors and other employees in dealing with an incident of workplace violence. Some behaviors require immediate police or security involvement, others constitute actionable misconduct and require disciplinary action, and others indicate an immediate need for an EAP referral.

On the other hand, it is seldom (if ever) advisable to rely on what are inappropriately referred to as "profiles" or "early warning signs" to predict violent behavior. Profiles often suggest people with certain characteristics, such as loners and men in their forties, are potentially violent. This kind of categorization will not help predict violence, and it can lead to unfair and destructive stereotyping. The same can be said of reliance on early warning signs that include descriptions of problem situations such as someone who is in therapy, had a death in the family, suffers from mental illness, or is facing a reduction in force.

Everyone experiences stress, loss, or illness at some point in life. All but a very few people weather these storms without resorting to violence. Supervisors should, of course, be trained to deal with the kinds of difficulties mentioned here, such as bereavement or mental illness. However, this training should focus on supporting the employee in the workplace, and not in the context of or on the potential for workplace violence.

When an analysis of indicators for increased risk of violence is paired with a review of risk mitigating factors, the threat assessment team should be alert to the situation in which the subject appears to have nothing to lose. For those individuals, the fear of disciplinary action or even dismissal or incarceration is no longer a deterrent.

There are some violence risk instruments, normally used by trained mental health professionals, available to agencies concerned with the possibility of workplace violence. The Historical Clinical Risk Management (HCR)-20[10], is an evidence-based instrument. Originally designed as a research tool, it can be useful as an applied device for assuring that all of the evidence-based risk factors are considered by the threat assessment team.

The Workplace Assessment of Violence Risk (WAVR)-21 (revised) is a proprietary instrument.[11] It is believed the WAVR-21 is the only workplace violence assessment tool currently marketed that is based upon current violence risk research and has been subjected to tests of statistical reliability. While the WAVR-21 is based upon the same body of research evidence as the HCR-20, it has the advantage of helping the threat assessment team to document review of not only risk factors but also risk mitigating factors. In addition, the WAVR-21 helps the threat assessment team track risk factors and risk mitigating factors that are dynamic in nature.

The authors specify the WAVR-21 should only be used by qualified test users. Furthermore, neither the HCR-20 nor the WAVR-21 should be considered a psychological test.

4.3.3. Training

Training for all agency personnel is an important part of any workplace violence prevention and response program. The training may differ based upon the target audience and type of employee groups, but, at a minimum, agencies should provide initial and recurring training on the following topics to all current employees, newly hired employees, supervisors, and managers:

- An overview of the various aspects and types of workplace violence;
- Symptoms and behaviors often associated with those who commit the violent behavior;
- Security hazards found in the organization's workplace;
- The organization's workplace violence prevention policies and procedures;
- Reporting requirements and processes;
- Specialized training on creating a positive work environment and developing effective teams;
- Training to improve awareness of cultural differences (diversity);
- Tips for protecting oneself and fellow coworkers;
- Response plan, communication, and alarm procedures; and
- Supervisory training in conducting a peaceful separation from service.

One example of a training program is the VHA's Prevention and Management of Disruptive Behavior (PMDB) employee education program.[12] PMDB utilizes a tiered approach to training that maps onto the results of a comprehensive workplace violence risk assessment and is generally well-received by the VHA's individual facilities.

Such an approach allows the VHA's individual medical centers to tailor their training programs to address the unique needs of their own diverse workforce.

PMDB is organized into four levels of training:

- Level I: Violence Prevention Awareness Training (1.5 hours on-line, Web-based training). Appropriate as a curriculum element in new employee orientation training.

- Level II: Observational and Verbal De-Escalation Skills (4 hours face-to-face training). Appropriate for employees assessed to be at low risk for workplace violence and/or for employees whose job duties require excellence in customer service interactions.
- Level III: Personal Safety Skills (4 hours of face-to-face training). Appropriate for employees who would benefit from having knowledge of basic self-protection and physical attack evasion and escape techniques. The combination of Level II and Level III training is appropriate for employees assessed to be at moderate risk for workplace violence.
- Level IV: Therapeutic Containment Skills (4 hours of face-to-face training). Appropriate for employees who may need to contain physically disruptive individuals in order to protect themselves and others from serious injury. The combination of Levels II, III, and IV training is appropriate for employees assessed to be at high risk for workplace violence.

Levels I, II, and III of the PMDB program may be adapted for use in any Federal agency. Level IV might be appropriate for employees of any Federal agency who at times may have to safely, physically constrain patients, inmates, or customers without intentionally utilizing the infliction of pain to effect containment.

Management's commitment at all levels is an important concept to communicate during the training. The presence of senior management at training sessions will increase the visibility and credibility of the organization's top-level commitment to preventing workplace violence. Training should also be provided to affected employees whenever management is made aware of a new or previously unrecognized hazard and to employees given new job assignments for which specific workplace security training for that job assignment has not previously been provided.

Training sessions conducted by the agency's EAP, security, and employee relations staffs are particularly helpful, enabling employees to get to know experts within the agency who can help them when potentially violent situations arise. Employees and supervisors seek assistance at a much earlier stage when they personally know the agency officials who can help.

Providing appropriate training informs employees management will take threats seriously, encourages employees to report incidents, and demonstrates management's commitment to deal with reported incidents. The following are types of training that proved effective in preventing violence and other threatening behavior.

4.3.3.1. Employee Training

All employees should know how to report incidents of violent, intimidating, threatening, and other disruptive behavior. All employees should also be provided with phone numbers for quick reference during a crisis or an emergency.

In addition, workplace violence prevention training for employees should follow a specific curriculum and lesson plan and may include topics such as:

- Explanation of the agency's workplace violence policy or program;
- Encouragement to report incidents;
- Ways of preventing or diffusing volatile situations or aggressive behavior;
- How to deal with hostile persons;
- How to identify and respond to behavior brought about by medical conditions, such as the onset of diabetic coma or the abuse of drugs;
- Managing anger;
- Techniques and skills to resolve conflicts;
- Stress management, relaxation techniques, wellness training;
- Security procedures, e.g. the location and operation of safety devices such as alarm systems;
- Personal security measures; and
- Programs operating within the agency that can assist employees in resolving conflicts, e.g. the Employee Assistance Program, the ombudsman, and mediation.

OSHA recommends employees in health care and social services organizations should receive formal instruction on the specific safety and security hazards associated with their particular job or facility. Detailed information is available in OSHA's *Guidelines for Preventing Workplace Violence for Health Care and Social Service Workers*. (See Appendix A for website and ordering information.)

NIOSH also discusses the importance of training tailored to the specific risks in the employee's workplace. NIOSH's publication *Violence in the Workplace: Risk Factors and Prevention Strategies* discusses clearly identifiable workplace risk factors, such as dealing with the public, and emphasizes that training will be more useful and credible when it addresses risk factors specific to job tasks or locations. (See Appendix A for website and ordering information.)

The Department of Homeland Security (DHS) initiated a training program called the Physical Security Outreach Program that addresses crime prevention as well as workplace violence awareness training. In addition, the Federal Emergency Management Agency hosts on its Web site an online course titled *IS-106.13 Workplace Violence Awareness Training 2013.*[13]

The training program, including a plan for emergency evacuation, should be designed and practiced. The evacuation plan should include not only procedures for getting workers out of a building, office, or plant, but some method for those evacuated to assemble or check in to determine who is safe and who may still be missing. Evacuation plans should include provisions for employees with disabilities: for example, ensuring hearing-impaired employees receive warnings and a system for safely evacuating anyone who uses a wheelchair.

The amount and frequency of retraining and response drills -- reinforcing skills competency -- is a determination also driven by the needs of the employees based upon the results of the workplace violence risk assessment. At a minimum, it is suggested skill competency assessments be done at least once every two years and face-to-face retraining every four years. Individual work groups often request training at more frequent intervals (e.g. annually) and such requests should be enthusiastically honored.

4.3.3.2. Supervisor Training

In addition to the training suggested above, special attention should be paid to general supervisor training. The same approaches that create a healthy, productive workplace can also help prevent potentially violent situations. It is important that supervisor training include basic leadership skills such as setting clear standards, addressing employee problems promptly, conscientiously using the probationary period, performance counseling, discipline, and other management tools. These interventions can keep difficult situations from turning into major problems. Supervisors do not need to be experts on violent behavior, but they do need to be willing and knowledgeable about how to seek advice from experts.

Some agencies include training on workplace violence as part of general supervisor training, some conduct separate training sessions on workplace violence, and some include it in crisis management training. Regardless of the approach taken, supervisor training should cover:

- Ways to encourage employees to report incidents that made them feel threatened for any reason by anyone inside or outside the organization;
- Skills in behaving compassionately and supportively towards employees who report incidents;
- Skills in taking disciplinary actions;
- Basic skills in handling crisis situations;
- Basic emergency procedures; and
- How to ensure appropriate screening of pre-employment references is completed.

Training sessions conducted by the agency's EAP, security, and employee relations staffs are particularly helpful, enabling employees to get to know experts within the agency who can help when potentially violent situations arise.

4.3.3.3. Incident Response Team Training

The members of the incident response team need to be competent in their own professions, and they need to know when to call for outside resources. Participating in programs and training sessions sponsored by government and professional organizations, reading professional journals and other literature, and networking with others in the profession are all helpful in gaining knowledge about dealing with workplace violence situations.

Team members also need to understand enough about each other's roles to allow them to work together effectively. Response team training should allow discussion of policies, legal constraints, technical vocabulary, and other considerations that each profession brings to the interdisciplinary group. Chapter 5 of this guide will introduce team members to key issues in professions other than their own.

Much of the incident response team training can be accomplished by practicing responses to different scenarios of workplace violence. The case studies in Appendix A of this guide are intended for this purpose. Practice exercises help departmental and agency personnel understand each other's responses to various situations to eliminate confusion or misunderstanding during an actual incident. In addition, practice exercises prepare the staff to conduct the supervisory training suggested above. Use practice exercises to see how the incident response team would deal with different situations.

Distinguishing the appropriate response training to the sources of threats represents a critical planning function as composition and applicable rules may differ dramatically. For example, patients who threaten or attack providers still have a provider-patient relationship: laws, regulations, and other patient care practice topics will influence both composition and response framework. Corrections and educational institutions have their own set of processes. Threats by co-workers involve administrative operations, underlie OPM regulations and Federal administration laws, and in most settings are driven by administrative oversight.

The team members also need to consult regularly with other personnel within the organization who may be involved in dealing with potentially violent situations. Those who are consulted on an ad hoc basis should receive some level of training as well.

4.3.4. Pre-Employment Screening

Pre-employment screening is an important part of workplace violence prevention. Prior to hiring an employee, the agency should check with its personnel and legal departments, if necessary, to determine what pre-employment screening techniques (such as interview questions, background and reference checks, and drug testing) are appropriate for the position under consideration and are consistent with Federal laws and regulations. EO 10450 and Homeland Security Presidential Directive 12 (HSPD-12) require a background investigation for Federal employees, contractors, and affiliates.

4.3.4.1. The Hiring Process

Because individuals who exhibit violent or bullying behavior usually have a history of such actions, a thorough hiring process can serve as one important step in helping prevent violence in the workplace. Agencies should make use of three vital tools during the hiring process: a face-to-face interview with the applicant, an assertive check of work references, and use of a probationary period for new employees.

A face-to-face interview can provide some sense of how the applicant interacts with people, responds to problems and unfamiliar environments, and handles other workplace challenges. However, since an interview is only a snapshot of behavior, some applicants may be able to deceive even a seasoned hiring manager and conceal possible future performance issues behind a well-rehearsed, seemingly professional appearance.

If the applicant is suitable based on the interview, the hiring authority should perform a thorough, comprehensive check of past references and other background information. Previous employers, supervisors, colleagues, and subordinates can often provide valuable insight into the applicant's personality and behavior; past performance is often an accurate predictor of future success. As a precaution, employers must be alert because the reference list is usually provided by the applicant, who is not likely to list persons who will provide unfavorable reports. In addition, most bullying behavior is covert and typically is not reported officially, so the previous employer/supervisor may not be aware of such behavior. An additional item worth noting is that many previous employers will only provide an acknowledgement of employment. Therefore, a complete check of the applicant's work history, including their military service, and a check of any possible criminal record, should also impact the hiring decision.

If after the interview and reference check the decision is made to move forward and hire the individual, proper use of a probationary period is in the best interest of both the new employee and Federal employer. This allows time for the employee, supervisor, and other staff members to determine whether the employee can perform the job. The U.S. Merit Systems Protection Board's (MSPB's) August 2005 report, *The Probationary Period: A Critical Assessment Opportunity*, provides additional information.

4.3.4.2. Challenges to the Hiring Process

The processes of interviewing the applicant, checking references, and assessing adequacies during the probationary period are standard management procedures. However, on occasion, one or more of the steps is omitted or not thoroughly completed, thereby likely increasing the possibility of allowing a violent applicant into the workplace. Various factors can tempt managers to circumvent or omit one or more steps in the hiring process.

Among these factors:

- Vacant positions can create hardship for the organization, causing missed deadlines, increasing the workload on the remaining employees, and increasing the difficulty of accommodating leave requests.
- Managers may rely on their "intuitive ability" to spot the "real person" under the polite facade and choose to base the hiring decision on an interview alone.
- The legalities surrounding background checks and interviews may intimidate some managers and lead them to avoid both processes. Federal Government Executive Order 10450 and Homeland Security Presidential Directive 12 require a background investigation for employees, contractors, and affiliates.

- Those checking references may not be experienced at assertively probing in the questioning of former employers, superiors, colleagues, and subordinates.

4.3.4.3. Resources and Support

Senior management should be made aware of the challenges their hiring personnel face during the hiring process. Managers also need to use the resources available to them in departments such as human resources, Equal Employment Opportunity, and general counsel. Professionals from these departments can advise managers on how to conduct a thorough and legal evaluation of the applicant. The guidance from these subject matter experts can reduce managers' liability and help navigate the hiring process thoroughly and efficiently.

4.3.5. Security Measures

Maintaining a physically safe workplace is part of any good prevention program. Agency facilities use a variety of security measures to help ensure safety. These include:

- Employee photo identification badges (should be constantly worn in plain sight); On-site guard services and/ or individually coded card keys for access to buildings and areas within buildings according to individual needs; and
- Guard enforced assistance in registering, badge issuing, and directing visitors in larger facilities.
- Appendix A contains additional suggestions for preventive security measures and resources for obtaining additional information.

4.3.6. Using Alternative Dispute Resolution as a Preventive Strategy

Some agencies use ombudsman programs, facilitation, mediation, and other methods of alternative dispute resolution (ADR) as preventive strategies in their workplace violence programs. ADR approaches often involve a neutral third party who can assist disputing parties in resolving disagreements. ADR is most helpful in workplace violence programs at the point when a problem first surfaces: i.e., before an employee's conduct rises to a level that warrants disciplinary action. The following is a short description of some ADR techniques agencies found useful in dealing with potential workplace violence problems at the very earliest stages.

4.3.6.1. Ombudsmen

Ombudsmen are individuals who rely on a number of techniques to resolve workplace disputes. These techniques include counseling, mediating, conciliating, and fact-finding. Usually, when an ombudsman receives a complaint, he or she interviews the parties, reviews available information and policies, and offers options to the disputants. Ombudsmen do not typically impose solutions. The effectiveness of the ombudsman lies in his or her problem-solving ability. Generally, an individual not accepting an option offered by the ombudsman is free to pursue a remedy using another forum for dispute resolution.

4.3.6.2. Facilitation

Facilitation techniques improve the flow of information in a meeting between parties to a dispute. The term "facilitator" is often used interchangeably with the term "mediator," but a facilitator does not typically become as involved in the substantive issues as does a mediator. The facilitator focuses more on the process involved in resolving a matter. Facilitation is most appropriate when the intensity of the parties' emotions about the issues in dispute are low to moderate, the parties or issues are not extremely polarized, or the parties have enough trust in each other that they can work together to develop a mutually acceptable solution.

4.3.6.3. Mediation

Mediation uses an impartial and neutral third party who has no decision-making authority. The objective of this intervention is to assist the parties in voluntarily reaching an acceptable resolution of issues in dispute. Mediation is useful in highly polarized disputes where the parties are either unable to initiate a productive dialogue, or, in cases where the parties have been talking and have reached a seemingly insurmountable impasse.

A mediator, like a facilitator, makes primarily procedural suggestions regarding how parties can reach agreement. A mediator may occasionally suggest some substantive options as a means of encouraging the parties to expand the range of possible resolutions under consideration. A mediator often works with the parties individually to explore acceptable resolution options or to develop proposals that might move the parties closer to resolution.

4.3.6.4. Interest-Based Problem Solving

Interest-based problem solving is a technique that creates effective solutions while improving the relationship between the parties. The process separates the person from the problem, explores all interests to define issues clearly, brainstorms possibilities and opportunities, and uses a mutually agreed upon standard to reach a solution. It is often used in collective bargaining between labor and management in place of traditional, position-based bargaining. However, as a technique, it can be effectively applied in many contexts where two or more parties are seeking to reach agreement.

4.3.6.5. Peer Review

Peer Review is a problem solving process whereby an employee takes a dispute to a panel of fellow employees and managers for a decision. The decision may or may not be binding on the employee and/or the employer, depending on the conditions of the particular process. If it is not binding on the employee, he or she would be able to seek relief in traditional forums for dispute resolution if dissatisfied with the decision under peer review. The principal objective of the method is to resolve disputes early before they become formal complaints or grievances. For a resource about alternative dispute resolution techniques, please see Appendix A.

4.3.6.6. Termination of Employment

Termination may be appropriate, but doing so in the heat of the moment without any time for evaluation or preparation may be precisely the wrong thing to do. Any removal or employment termination process must follow all established agency procedures. The manager should strive to maintain an atmosphere of dignity and respect and should use all available resources including professional assistance in assessing the potential physical and psychological consequences. If the removal is due to downsizing, restructuring, or some other business issue, managers should not increase the employee's distress by treating him or her as potentially dangerous. Instead, the manager should treat the employee with respect, be supportive of the employee's job search, and ensure the employee is aware of the available resources such as placement services, job search training, and career counseling. In the rare instance when someone could become violent, properly trained coworkers are likely to notice behavioral changes signaling the need for more focused attention.

If the removal is "for cause," particularly if it is due to bullying or violent behavior, other forms of misconduct, or illegal actions, there may be potential for violence. Training supervisors to recognize the warning signs and make use of available resources can help them defuse the potential for workplace violence. Also, while most EAPs provide services to current employees, allowing recently terminated employees to access the program may be beneficial.

4.4. Conclusion to Planning, Prevention, and Response

This document provides information related to the establishment of practical workplace violence prevention and response and facility preparedness programs within the Federal government framework. Recognizing that each government facility is unique in its physical environment, the goal of this document is to assist Federal agencies in developing and implementing agency specific workplace violence prevention programs. Agency leaders will be able to use this document and the reference documents (listed under Resources) to create sustainable programs. One sample of a checklist for creating a workplace violence prevention and response program is provided as follows:

WORKPLACE VIOLENCE PREVENTION and RESPONSE PROGRAM CHECKLIST [*SAMPLE]*	Completion Date *(mm/dd/yy)*	Annual Audit Date *(mm/dd/yy)*
Written workplace violence prevention policy statement		
Physical preparedness plan		
Workplace violence risk/threat assessment		
Awareness program that includes domestic violence at work		
Hiring process that includes background checks		
EAP		
Work/life program		
Alternative dispute resolution program		
Workplace violence prevention training		
Procedures for reporting workplace violence		
Communication procedures that include field workers		
Evacuation, shelter-in-place, and deep shelter procedures and drills		
Security plans for responding to violence		
Employee support services for those involved in violent incidents		
Incident investigation procedures		
Review plan for continuous improvement		

5.0. Investigations, Assessments, and Other

The information in this chapter provides guidance for the agency planning group that may be comprised of members of an agency's human resources, EAP, legal, and security offices as well as representatives of the agency's Facility Security Committee (FSC), union(s) (if present) and senior management among others. The information is neither technical information for professional investigators nor a summary of fact-finding or investigating procedures. Rather, it is intended to provide the agency planning group with a general overview of fact-finding/investigating considerations. It is also important to note this chapter discusses investigations that are administrative inquiries distinct from criminal investigations.

5.1. Section 1: Investigations

> "I can't work here anymore.
> I'm afraid he may actually kill one of us."

The supervisor hears the details of the incident causing the employee to feel threatened. Now the supervisor has to do something. The incident cannot be ignored. It must be reported. Once reported, the members of the incident response team (along with the supervisor) must look into it.

5.1.1. Incident Investigation

Oftentimes, an incident investigation will be conducted by either trained internal staff and/or outside law enforcement at the same time as any post-trauma intervention.

The investigation can be particularly disturbing for employees who were personally involved in, witnessed, or knew coworkers involved in the workplace violence event. It is important the investigation be conducted in a professional and sensitive manner.

Investigators should:

- Visit the scene of the incident as soon as possible;
- Treat respectfully any evidence that needs to be preserved until the scene is cleared;
- Interview injured and threatened employees and witnesses;

- Remind witnesses who are being interviewed that the investigation's goal is to prevent future incidents;
- Inform witnesses of their rights;
- Inform witnesses they can refuse to answer questions and can stop the interview at any time;
- Examine the workplace for security risk factors associated with the incident, including any reports of inappropriate behavior by the perpetrator;
- Determine the cause of the incident;
- Take mitigating action to prevent the incident from recurring; and
- Record the findings and mitigating actions taken.

The information gathered during an incident investigation is invaluable in the effort to continuously improve workplace violence prevention and response and facility preparedness programs.

> As the agency begins its incident investigation, it is important to ensure actions taken by the agency during the investigation do not impede potential criminal prosecutions.

5.1.2. Understanding the Situation

As in all other serious administrative matters that come to the agency's attention, there is probably a want to learn more about what is going on in this situation. The needed information includes:

- **What** happened;
- **Who** was involved;
- **Where** did it happen;
- **When** did it happen;
- **Why** did it happen; and
- **How** did it happen?

5.1.3. What to Do next

Sometimes taking a few minutes for a cursory overview will give enough information to know what to do next. Of course, if there is imminent danger, law enforcement must be notified immediately. If there is no imminent danger, deciding what to do next will depend on agency procedures and the strategy/relationship developed ahead of time within the agency's Office of the

General Counsel, Office of Inspector General, and the law enforcement organization that has jurisdiction over the worksite. (For information on law enforcement, see Chapter 5, Section 5, sub-section 5.6.2.) In most Federal agencies, these offices are notified immediately when certain types of reports are made, and they advise team members (or agency officials) on how to proceed with the investigation of the case.

5.2. Section 2: Types of Investigations

Often, one of the first decisions to be made is whether to conduct an administrative or a criminal investigation. The answer will depend on whether the facts as presented indicate possible criminal behavior. Since arriving at a decision generally involves discussion with law enforcement personnel, the Office of the General Counsel (OGC), the Office of Inspector General (OIG), and employee relations specialists, it is imperative to coordinate efforts fully with these offices ahead of time. Also, as discussed below, an important point of these discussions is to ensure actions taken by an agency during an administrative investigation do not impede potential criminal prosecutions.

5.2.1. Administrative Investigations

5.2.1.1. Use a qualified investigator

If a decision is made to conduct an administrative investigation, it is important to use a qualified and experienced professional workplace violence investigator. The agency planning group should locate one or more such investigators before the need for an investigator arises. The agency probably has qualified administrative investigators, for example, in the OIG. Other places to look in the agency might be employee relations and security. In some agencies, these offices have their own investigators; in others, they contract with private investigators or utilize the services of investigators from other Federal agencies. In any case, they should be able to help locate trained, qualified administrative investigators ahead of time.

Additional considerations for the agency planning group, such as having well-defined agency policies on handling investigations, are discussed at the end of this section.

It is important to use an investigator who conducts the investigation in a fair and objective manner. The investigation should be conducive to developing truthful responses to issues that may surface. It must be conducted with full appreciation for the legal considerations that protect individual privacy. It is imperative to maintain an atmosphere of candor and propriety.

5.2.1.2. Ensure Criminal Prosecutions Are Not Compromised

Criminal prosecutions must not be compromised by actions taken during administrative investigations. It is necessary to ensure the administrative investigator, management, and all members of an incident response team understand actions taken during an administrative investigation may compromise potential criminal prosecutions. If the agency obtains statements from the subject of the investigation in the wrong way, the statements can impede or even destroy the ability to criminally prosecute the case. On the other hand, if handled correctly, statements made in administrative investigations could prove vital in subsequent criminal proceedings.

Therefore, in a case where a decision is made to conduct an administrative investigation and there is potential criminal liability, it is good practice to give the subject of the investigation what are usually called "non-custodial warnings and assurances." That is to say the person is given the option of participating in the interview after being warned that any statements he or she makes may be used against him or her in criminal proceedings. The option not to participate in the interview is exercised by the person's invocation of his or her Fifth Amendment right against self-incrimination. It should be noted that, since the person is not legally in custody, he or she is not entitled to an attorney.

If the investigator decides to compel the subject of an investigation to participate in an interview instead of being given an option to participate, then the investigator should give Kalkines[14] warning. This means the person is told: (1) he or she is subject to discharge for not answering; and (2) statements he or she makes (and the information gained as a result of these statements) cannot be used against him or her in criminal proceedings. Even if an investigator does not actually give Kalkines warning, if the investigator compels the subject to give a statement, the information in the statement (and the information gained as a result of the statement) cannot be used in criminal proceedings. Therefore, it may be advisable to only use this approach if there is a great degree of certainty the person being questioned will not be subject to criminal proceedings.

Since this may make criminal prosecution impossible, an investigator should never give Kalkines warning or compel statements from the subject of an investigation without the permission of the appropriate U. S. Attorney's or prosecutor's office. Such permission is usually obtained by the agency's OGC or OIG. Since this is an extremely complicated consideration, be sure to work closely with your OGC, OIG, and law enforcement organization. In potentially violent situations, it is often difficult to determine whether the misconduct is a criminal offense. If there is the slightest doubt, it is advisable to look into the situation.

5.2.1.3. Preparation and Procedures in Administrative Investigations

A thorough and professional investigative product is the result of significant preparation and quality procedures. Personally obtaining information from individuals will constitute a significant part of any investigation. An awareness of the skills and techniques necessary for effective interviewing is required. In preparing for and conducting investigations, experienced professional administrative investigators found the following approaches to be effective.

5.2.1.4. Reviewing Available Information

The investigator, after thoroughly reviewing the information that gave rise to the investigation, is probably ready to begin the investigation process. Discrepancies or deficiencies in the information should be noted so they can be addressed during the interviews.

5.2.1.5. Selecting an Interview Site

Since the investigator is conducting an official investigation, he or she should conduct as many interviews as possible in an official environment, i.e., in government work space (instead of restaurants, cars, or private homes). Privacy is the most important consideration in selection of an interview site. The investigator should guarantee the room will be available for the entire interview, so there is no disruption of the interview once it begins. The interview room should be comfortably furnished with as few distractions as possible.

5.2.1.6. Scheduling the Interview

Depending on the circumstances of the situation, the investigator may or may not want to contact the individual in advance. In either event, the investigator should advise the individual of the general nature and purpose of the interview. If the individual declines the interview, the investigator should attempt to dissuade the individual and, if unsuccessful, ascertain and record the reasons for the declination. If the individual fails to appear more than once for the interview, the investigator should follow whatever policy has been decided upon by the agency ahead of time.

5.2.1.7. Allowing the Presence of Additional Persons

There may be instances when the investigator or the individual being interviewed wishes to have an additional person present (for cases involving bargaining unit employees, see the discussion in the next section). Investigators sometimes prefer to have an agency representative present when interviewing the subject of the investigation. In any event, the investigator should follow whatever policy has been decided upon by the agency ahead of time.

5.2.1.8. Adhering to the Law Regarding Bargaining Unit Employees

The provisions of law set forth in 5 USC §7114(a) (2) (B), commonly known as "Weingarten[15]" rights, covers any examination of a bargaining unit employee by a representative of the agency in connection with an investigation.

If a bargaining unit employee reasonably believes an investigation may result in disciplinary action and requests union representation, the agency has three options:

- Immediately terminate the interview;
- Continue the interview with the employee's representative present; or
- Give the employee the option of proceeding with the interview without a representative or terminating the interview.

Since interpretation of this law is very complex, consult with your labor relations specialists or OGC when faced with such situations. Note: the law is currently unsettled as to whether Inspector General investigations are subject to 5 USC §7114(a) (2) (B).

5.2.1.9. Taking Notes

Since watching an investigator take notes can be intimidating to some people, it is important to establish rapport before beginning to take notes. The investigator should concentrate on observing the individual during the interview. Note taking should not unduly interfere with observation. Note taking materials should be positioned inconspicuously and not become a focus of attention. The investigator should learn and exercise the skill of taking adequate notes while still observing the individual and without distracting the person being interviewed. In some cases, it may even be useful to have a second investigator or other official present for the purposes of taking notes, corroboration of the statements given, and to ensure a third party is present to validate/invalidate claims if the subject accuses the interviewer of misconduct or prejudice during the interview.

Should note taking have a materially adverse effect on the interview process, the investigator may explain the purpose of note taking. The notes are intended for the investigator's use in preparing a report and are not a verbatim transcript of the interview. The investigator can modify or cease note taking so long as the information can be recorded in adequate detail after the interview.

5.2.1.10. Maintaining Control of the Interview

Questions developed ahead of time can be memorized, but they should never be read verbatim from a list or recited in a perfunctory manner. The investigator should know in advance the topics of concern to be covered. He/She should maintain a singleness of purpose during the interview and resist any efforts to shorten the interview or drift from topics of concern.

5.2.1.11. Developing Rapport

The investigator should have a comfortable style that projects professionalism and competence. His/Her style should generate rapport with the person being interviewed. An open approach that conveys a willingness to communicate generally fosters rapport. Rapport is evident when the individual appears comfortable with the investigator and is willing to confide personally sensitive information. Continuing rapport can oftentimes be maintained if the investigator does not become judgmental when disagreeable conduct or information is disclosed. The investigator who can project empathy when appropriate to do so often gains special insight but, at the same time, no investigator should get personally involved with the case.

5.2.1.12. Handling Hostility

If the investigator feels threatened by the individual being interviewed, the investigator should stop the interview and report the situation to the appropriate authorities.

Investigators may encounter argumentative individuals. When this type of hostility is encountered, the investigator can seek to defuse it by explaining the purpose of the interview and that the interview is a required part of the investigation. Reminding the interviewee that the investigator has full authority to conduct the interview and that the interviewee is required to cooperate may lessen the reluctance. (See, however, the discussion in section 5.2.1 regarding warnings that must be given when requiring the subject of an investigation to cooperate.)

Recognizing and acknowledging the person's hostility and the reason for it will sometimes let both parties reach the mutual understanding that the interview will proceed (whether or not the topics under discussion are related to the hostility).

If, after repeated attempts in various ways, an individual refuses to answer a specific question, the investigator should attempt to learn the reason. The investigator should record the refusal to answer any question and the reason. If the individual wants to terminate the interview, the investigator should attempt to learn the reason and to dissuade the individual by addressing the concerns. If the individual persists, the investigator should conclude the interview.

5.2.2. Interview Techniques

This section contains questioning, listening, and observation techniques and suggestions.

5.2.2.1. Questioning Techniques

Questioning usually proceeds from general areas to specific issues. For example, comments on the dates and location of the incident are usually obtained before comments on the circumstances surrounding the event.

The investigator should usually frame questions that require a narrative answer. Soliciting "Yes" or "No" responses restricts the individual from providing information. Such responses are helpful when summarizing or verifying information, but they should be avoided when seeking to elicit new information.

The investigator should use questioning techniques that result in the most productive responses from the person being investigated. This requires the investigator to exercise judgment based on observation of attitude, demeanor, and actions during the interview. These may change at times during the interview. The investigator should be continuously alert to such changes and should modify questioning techniques accordingly.

5.2.2.2. Non-confrontational approach

The non-confrontational approach is best. Here are some examples of the non-confrontational approach.

- If a person refuses to answer follow-up questions about an issue, the investigator notes the refusal to answer and moves on to the next area of questioning. However, the investigator then comes back to the issue later.
- If the person raises his or her voice in the interview, the investigator maintains a calm, level voice, or lowers his or her voice.

5.2.2.3. Direct and Non-direct Questions

A direct question calls for a factual or precise answer. Direct questions are ordinarily used when covering background data.

Here are some examples of direct questions:

- Who told you that he made a threat? When did you notice that he had a gun?
- What were the circumstances surrounding the argument?

Non-direct questions are usually more appropriate in discussing opinions and feelings because they allow more latitude in responding.

Here are some examples of non-direct questions:

- What led you to say that?
- What made that unusual?
- Has this happened before to anyone?
- What was your reaction when he yelled at you?

5.2.2.4. Assumptive Questions

Assumptive questions assume involvement in the activity under discussion. The investigator can use assumptive questions when involvement has already been admitted, either at some other time or earlier in the interview. Assumptive questions allow the investigator to assist the individual in describing the degree of involvement, particularly when it is difficult to respond in narrative. The investigator puts the individual at ease when using assumptive questions by demonstrating that the investigator is not shocked by the conduct being discussed.

Here are some examples of assumptive questions:

- Have you made similar statements to others?
- Is it fairly standard for you to carry a knife to work?

5.2.2.5. Summarizing Questions

Summarizing questions are used to verify what has been said in summary form. The investigator uses summarizing questions to give the individual an opportunity to hear what the investigator understood. In concluding each segment of the interview, the investigator should pause after asking a summarizing question to allow the individual to respond and verify, correct, disagree with, or amplify a previous response.

Here are some examples of summarizing questions:

- In other words, it was not what he said, but the tone of his voice, that scared you?
- You are telling me that you were only joking when you said you would blow up the place?
- Have I got this straight? You did not think he would actually carry out his threat?

5.2.2.6. Listening Techniques

Investigators should not be intent on listening for the end of an answer only so that they can get to the next question. If they do this, the meaning and sense of the answers will be ignored and lost. Careful attention to each response is what provides the basis for the next appropriate question, not a checklist of questions.

The person being interviewed may be signaling a problem with the area under discussion by not immediately responding to a question. The investigator should be patient and let the person respond. The urge to complete a statement for the person with an assumption of what the person was going to say should be suppressed.

Listen to the whole response for its substance, inferences, suggestions, or implications that there is more to be said or some qualification to the answer. Answers that are really non-answers, such as "that's about right," or "you know how it is," are not helpful because they are not definitive. Do not accept this type of response. Press for more specificity. Some people may attempt to avoid responding by blaming a faulty memory. Follow-up questions that can stimulate responses are: "Do you mean you are just not sure?", and, "But you remember something about it, don't you?"

Investigators should both listen and think intensely throughout the interview, measuring what is being said with what is already known. Compare new information to other statements made in the interview and any other information in the investigator's possession.

5.2.2.7. Observation Techniques

Questioning and listening are not the only communicative aspects of the interview. Actions may strengthen the credibility of the spoken word or contradict it. Body movement, gestures, and other observable manifestations may provide clues to truth and deception. The investigator should be alert to behavior changes throughout the interview and assess the significance of those changes. While no single behavior indicates truth or deception, clusters of behavior patterns may be valuable clues to the truth of what is being said. These patterns should prompt the investigator to pursue a certain or broader line of questioning.

5.2.3. Other Considerations for the Agency Planning Group

Here are other fact finding/investigating issues the agency planning group should address:

- Agency policy should be formulated ahead of time regarding such matters as no-shows for the interviews, whether to allow tape recording of the interviews, and whether to allow the presence of additional persons during the interviews. Policy should be based on sound legal analysis.
- Keep in mind the routine, administrative details cannot be ignored. Prior to beginning the actual investigation, the investigator should be given all administrative details, e.g., who gets the report and whom to contact regarding other administrative matters such as the investigator's pay, parking, and overtime.
- Consider giving the investigator the list of factors the MSPB will consider in making credibility determinations if the investigation leads to a case before the Board[16]. They are:
    - The witness' opportunity and capacity to observe the event or act in question;
    - The witness' character;
    - Any prior inconsistent statement by the witness;

- A witness' bias or lack of bias;
- The contradiction of the witness' version of events by other evidence or its consistency with other evidence;
- The inherent improbability of the witness' version of events; and
- The witness' demeanor.

Every step of the investigation should be objective, impartial, and unbiased. The investigative report will contain:

- Statements of witnesses; and
- Documentary evidence.

The investigative report generally does not include an analysis of the report.

- Both the investigator and the person who prepares the analysis of the report should be objective, impartial, and unbiased.
- Consider developing a letter signed by the agency head or high-level designated official authorizing the investigation and requiring employees to cooperate. (See, however, the information above regarding warnings to the subjects of administrative investigations when it is necessary to require cooperation.)
- Ensure all appropriate agency personnel are aware of the requirements discussed above regarding warnings when compelling statements from the subject of an administrative investigation.

Appendix A, Case Study 10 provides practical examples of some of the issues discussed in this section.

5.3. Section 3: Threat Assessment Assistance

5.3.1. Threat assessment

As the case studies in Appendix A illustrate, many cases involving threatening behavior can be handled expeditiously and effectively by a supervisor with the assistance of one or more members of the agency's incident response team. The security or law enforcement representative on the agency's team will ordinarily assess risks, often in consultation with the EAP and employee relations staff, and make recommendations for appropriate strategies and security measures to protect employees. However, it may be helpful for the agency's planning group to identify experts in threat assessment ahead of time in case a situation requires more expertise than team members can provide.

5.3.1.1. Gathering information

It is also a good idea to work out ahead of time who will gather the various types of information on an individual who makes a threat. Multiple sources of information need to be consulted to better understand the individual's behavior.

In some cases, the agency's incident response team can collect current and reliable information (including an investigative report) and then consult with a threat assessment professional to develop options for managing the situation. In other cases, the agency's incident response team uses a threat assessment professional to conduct the initial investigation, assess the risks, and make recommendations for managing the situation.

Threat assessment investigations differ from criminal or administrative investigations in that the purpose of the threat assessment investigation is to provide guidance on managing the situation in a way that protects the employees.

5.3.1.2. Threat Assessment Resources

Threat assessment is an evolving technical field. It is important to find a qualified professional to assist you if the need arises. Several Federal agencies have experienced threat assessment professionals within their organizations; some have threat management units within their criminal investigative services. If the agency does not have access to such professionals, law enforcement agencies (such as FPS, FBI, and state and local police) may be able to assist in identifying experts in threat assessment.

If the agency uses a threat assessment professional who is outside the organization, ensure the individual is aware of all relevant Federal laws and regulations. For example, as explained in Chapter 5, Sub-Section 5.4.4, Federal regulations in 5 CFR § 339 prohibit ordering a psychological examination under most circumstances and the threat assessment professional thus must understand the limits of the inquiry. Another example is the Privacy Act provisions of 5 USC §552a that include obligations for guarding personal data. The Association of Threat Assessment Professionals (ATAP) is an international multidisciplinary association that includes members from Federal, state, and local law enforcement agencies; behavioral scientists working in the violence assessment and management arena; and corporate security personnel. The purpose of ATAP, a non-profit organization, is to promote research on violence, to develop ethical practices in the field of threat assessment and management to promote best practices, and to encourage networking across customary discipline boundaries.

ATAP published a document titled *Risk Assessment Guidelines Elements for Violence: Considerations for Assessing the Risk of Future Violent Behavior*[17]". In addition, ATAP published ethical guidelines available to members. A large number of Federal agencies are already represented among the ATAP membership.

5.3.2. Excerpts from Threat Assessment: An Approach to Prevent Targeted Violence

> The remainder of this section, 5.3.2, consists of excerpts from a research brief on the topic of threat assessment issued by the U. S. Department of Justice's National Institute of Justice. The brief, titled *Threat Assessment: An Approach to Prevent Targeted Violence*[18] and written by Robert A. Fein, Ph. D., Bryan Vossekuil, and Gwen A. Holden, explains the functions of a threat assessment program, including the investigation, risk assessment, and case management components.
>
> This research brief can be especially helpful for an agency's planning group to gain an understanding of the process of conducting threat assessments so that group members can better identify experts in threat assessment before they are actually needed and learn how they can coordinate efforts with them when the need arises.
>
> **NOTE**: The excerpts in this section address "targeted violence." However, targeted violence is the least common type of violence in many Federal agencies. While Federal agencies are sometimes the targets of predators, the agencies need to be fully aware of daily "violence" that disrupts the workplace and can be just as dangerous.

Traditional law enforcement activities aim to apprehend and prosecute perpetrators of violence after the commission of their crimes. In most circumstances, the primary responsibility of law enforcement professionals is to determine whether a crime has been committed, conduct an investigation to identify and apprehend the perpetrator, and gather evidence to assist prosecutors in a criminal trial. However, when police officers are presented with information about a possible future violent crime, their responsibilities, authority, and investigative tools and approaches are less clear. "Threat assessment" is the term used to describe the set of investigative and operational techniques that can be used by law enforcement professionals to identify, assess, and manage the risks of targeted violence and its potential perpetrators.

Individuals utter threats for many reasons, only some of which involve intention or capacity to commit a violent act. However, a person can present a grave threat without articulating it. The distinction between making and posing a threat is important.

- Some persons who make threats ultimately pose threats;
- Many persons who make threats do not pose threats; and
- Some persons who pose threats never make threats.

Postponing action until a threat is made can detract attention from investigation of factors more relevant to the risk of violence.

Data from two studies suggest that at least some "approachers"—and attackers—of public officials/figures show an interest in more than one target.[19] U.S. Secret Service experience indicates that a number of would-be presidential assassins, such as Arthur Bremer and John Hinckley, considered several targets, and changed targets, before finally making an attack. Data on relationship stalking murders and workplace violence murders point to suicide, as well as homicide, as a possible outcome.[20] These examples suggest that, in some cases, the perpetrator may ultimately become his or her own final target.

The threat of sanctions, such as a long prison sentence, may not deter a person who desperately desires revenge or is prepared to die to achieve his/her objective. Passage of enforceable laws that define and prohibit behaviors presaging violent attacks is one important step in preventing such attacks. All fifty states, five U.S. territories, and the District of Columbia passed anti-stalking laws. In addition, authorities in some jurisdictions are reviewing various threat and harassment laws to determine applicability to threat-of-violence situations. However, laws by themselves are unlikely to prevent stalking, workplace, or public figure-centered violence; law enforcement and security professionals must also know how to identify, evaluate, and manage persons at risk of committing these violent acts.

5.3.2.1. Fundamental Principles of Threat Assessment

Notwithstanding the growing importance of threat assessment for law enforcement and security professionals, systematic thinking and guidance in this area is lacking in many organizations. Some law enforcement and security communities currently do not have clearly articulated processes or procedures to steer their actions when they are made aware of threat-of-violence subjects and situations. Without guidelines for making threat assessments, otherwise competent law enforcement professionals may be less thoughtful and thorough than required in handling such incidents. To fill the void, this report presents four fundamental principles underlying threat assessment investigation and management. A model and process for conducting comprehensive threat assessment investigations follows thereafter.

- Violence is a process, as well as an act. Violent behavior does not occur in a vacuum. Careful analysis of violent incidents shows violent acts often are the culmination of long-developing, identifiable trails of problems, conflicts, disputes, and failures.
- Violence is the product of an interaction among three factors: the individual who takes violent action; stimulus or triggering conditions that lead the subject to see violence as an option, "way out," or solution to problems or life situation; and a setting that facilitates or permits the violence, or at least does not stop it from occurring.
- A key to investigation and resolution of threat assessment cases is identification of the subject's "attack-related" behaviors. Perpetrators of targeted acts of violence engage in discrete behaviors that precede and are linked to their attacks; they consider, plan, and prepare before engaging in violent actions.
- Threatening situations are more likely to be successfully investigated and managed if other agencies and systems—both within and outside law enforcement or security organizations—are recognized and used to help solve problems presented by a given case. Examples of such systems are those employed by prosecutors; courts; probation, corrections, social service, and mental health agencies; employee assistance programs; victim's assistance programs; and community groups.

5.3.2.2. Functions of a Threat Assessment Program

The three major functions of a threat assessment program are (1) identification of a potential perpetrator, (2) assessment of the risks of violence posed by a given perpetrator at a given time, and (3) management of both the subject and the risks that he or she presents to a given target.

5.3.2.3. Identifying the Perpetrator

The process of identifying a potential perpetrator involves: (1) defining criteria that could lead to a person becoming a subject of a threat assessment investigation; (2) determining the areas within the law enforcement or security organization responsible for receiving information about possible subjects and conducting threat assessment investigations; (3) notifying those individuals and organizations that might come in contact with—or know of—potential subjects about the existence of a threat assessment program; and (4) educating notified individuals and organizations about the criteria for bringing a concern about potential violence to the attention of investigators.

5.3.2.4. Assessing the Risks

The second goal of a threat assessment program is to evaluate the risks persons under suspicion may pose to particular targets. Risk assessment involves two primary functions: investigation and evaluation.

5.3.2.5. Investigation

The primary objective of a risk assessment investigation is to gather information on a subject and on potential targets. Multiple sources of information should be consulted to learn about a subject's behavior, interests, and state of mind at various points in time.

- Personal interviews with the subject;
- Material created or possessed by the subject, including journals and letters, and materials collected by the subject, such as books and magazines, that may relate to the investigation;
- Persons who know or have known the subject, including family members, friends, coworkers, supervisors, neighbors, landlords, law enforcement officers, social service or mental health staff, and previous victims of unacceptable behavior (including violence) committed by the subject; and
- Record or archival information, including police, court, probation, and correctional records; mental health and social service records; and notes made by those aware of the subject's interest in a particular target, such as security personnel, managers, victims, or colleagues.

5.3.2.6. Information About the Subject

At the beginning of a threat assessment investigation, it is important to secure detailed descriptions of the subject's behaviors and actions that prompted other persons to notice the subject. The kinds of information useful for threat assessment include data about overwhelmingly or unbearably stressful experiences and the subject's ability to cope at such times. Behavioral data about the subject's motives, intentions, and capacities is critical.

Of particular importance is information about attack-related behaviors:

- The subject expressed interest in possible targets, including particular, identifiable targets;
- The subject communicated with or about potential targets;
- The subject considered and/or attempted to harm self or others;
- The subject secured or practiced with weapons; and
- The subject followed or approached potential targets, either with or without weapons, at events or occasions.

5.3.2.7. Interviewing the Subject

Whether to interview the subject of a threat assessment investigation can be a key question, and the decision depends on several factors:

- The investigator's need for information;
- The facts leading to initiation of investigation;
- The investigator's legal standing in relation to the subject;
- The resources available to the investigator;
- The investigator's training and experience in interviewing;
- The stage of the investigation; and
- The investigator's strategy for resolving the case.

A decision to interview a subject should be made on the basis of case facts. Generally, after a face-to-face contact between subject and target or the subject communicated a threat to the target, an interview is a good idea. An interview under such circumstances may have several goals. It may signal that the subject's behavior has been noticed, permit the subject's story to be related to a third party, gather information forming the basis for corroboration, and provide an opportunity for communicating the subject's behavior is unwelcome, unacceptable, and must cease.

Any interview is a vehicle for gathering information about the subject used to assess the threat a subject poses and to manage the threat. Therefore, threat assessment interviews are most productive if conducted respectfully and professionally. The task of the investigator is twofold: (1) to gather information about the subject's thinking, behavior patterns, and activities regarding the target(s) and (2) to encourage change in the subject's behavior. By showing an interest in the subject's life that is neither unduly friendly nor harsh, an investigator can increase the likelihood of the interview's success.

In some cases, however, an interview may intensify the subject's interest in the target or increase the risk of lethal behavior. For example, a desperate and suicidal subject, self-perceived as having been abandoned, who has been stalking a former partner, may sense time is running out and be prompted by an interview to engage in more extreme behavior before "they put me away." In such circumstances, the investigator may need to expend additional resources, perhaps increasing security for the target, arranging hospitalization or arrest of the subject, or monitoring or screening the subject. Subject interviews, therefore, should be considered and conducted within the context of overall investigative strategy.

5.3.2.8. Information About the Target

A man, who over days and weeks, follows a secretary whom he met once but has no relationship, appears to have picked out a potential target. An employee, fired by a manager whom he blames for discriminating against him and causing the breakup of his family, has told former coworkers that he will "get even." Once again, a potential target appears to have been selected. To prevent violence, the threat assessment investigator requires information on the targeted individual. Relevant questions about the target might include the following:

- Are potential targets identifiable or does it appear the subject, if considering violence, has not yet selected targets for possible attack?
- Is the potential target well known to the subject? Is the subject acquainted with a targeted individual's work and personal lifestyle, patterns of living, or daily comings and goings?
- Is the potential target vulnerable to an attack? Does the targeted individual possess resources to arrange for physical security? What change in the target's lifestyle or living arrangements could make attack by the subject more difficult or less likely, e.g., is the targeted individual planning to move, spend more time at home, or take a new job?

- Is the target afraid of the subject? Is the targeted individual's degree of fear shared by family, friends, and/or colleagues?
- How sophisticated or naive is the targeted individual about the need for caution? How able is the individual to communicate a clear and consistent "I want no contact with you" message to the subject?

5.3.2.9. Evaluation

A two-stage process is suggested to evaluate information gathered about the subject and the potential target(s). In the first stage, information is evaluated for evidence of conditions and behaviors consistent with planning an attack. The second stage of evaluation seeks to determine whether the subject appears to be moving toward or away from an attack. After analyzing the available data, the threat assessor is left with these questions:

- Does it appear more or less likely violent action will be directed by the subject against the target(s)? What specific information and reasoning lead to this conclusion?
- How close is the subject to attempting an attack? What thresholds, if any, were crossed (e.g., the subject violated court orders, made a will, given away personal items, expressed willingness to die or to be incarcerated)?
- What might change in the subject's life to increase or decrease the risk of violence? What might change in the target's situation to increase or decrease the risk of violence?

5.3.2.10. Case Management

The first component of threat assessment case management involves developing a plan that moves the subject away from regarding violence against the target as a viable option. Such a plan is likely to draw on resources from systems within the threat assessment unit's parent organization, as well as those outside it. The second component is plan implementation. The best developed and supported case management plan will be of little use in preventing violence if the plan is not implemented and monitored. The plan must remain flexible to accommodate changes in the subject's life and circumstances. The final management component is formal closing of the case.

5.3.2.11. Case Management Development

Once an evaluator determines a given subject presents a risk of violence to a targeted individual, the next task is to develop a plan to manage the subject and the risk. The evaluator then proceeds to identify those internal and external systems that may be helpful in managing the problems presented by the subject. In certain situations, such as those in which the subject is stalking an identifiable target in a jurisdiction with an enforceable and effective anti-stalking law, the best way to prevent violence and minimize harm to the targeted individual may be to prosecute the case vigorously.

A good relationship between threat assessment investigators and prosecutors can influence the priority assigned to the case and the extent to which prosecutorial and judicial processes facilitate its resolution. Such relationships also may affect the court's disposition of the case, including sentencing of a convicted offender.

Even conviction and imprisonment, however, do not guarantee the target will be safe from the subject. If the subject is unable or unwilling to let go of the idea of a relationship with the target, or if the subject attributes the pains and misfortunes of his or her life to the targeted individual, it may make sense to consider strategies in which the subject is encouraged to change the direction, or intensity, of his/her interest. A subject engaged in activities that bring success and satisfaction is less likely to remain preoccupied with a failed relationship. Family, friends, neighbors, or associates may play a role in suggesting and supporting changes in the subject's thinking and behavior. In addition, mental health and social service staff may be of great assistance in aiding the subject to formulate more appropriate goals and develop skills and strengths likely to result in life successes.

At least one aspect of a case management plan concerns the target. If the subject is to be prohibited from contact with the target, the target needs to understand what to do (i.e., whom to call and how to contact the official handling the case) if the subject initiates direct or indirect contact.

5.3.2.12. Case Management Implementation

The most carefully crafted plan will have little effect if it remains in the investigator's files and is not translated into action. Although no procedures or techniques can guarantee that a subject of comprehensive threat assessment will not attempt violent action toward a target, two activities are known to help reduce the risk of violence, and, in the instance of a bad outcome, assist the threat assessment team in any post-incident review.

First, documentation of data and reasoning at every stage of a threat assessment investigation is essential. Undocumented or poorly documented information gathering and analysis is suspect in and of themselves, and they provide little foundation for review or for efforts to learn from—and improve on— experience. Without clear documentation, investigators are left with only their recollections that can be both partial and faulty and are subject to criticism as retrospective reconstruction. A carefully and comprehensively documented record may be criticized for imperfect data gathering or flawed analysis, but such a record also demonstrates both thoughtfulness and good faith—critical questions in any post-incident review.

Second, consultation at every major stage of the threat assessment process can be a significant case management tool. Consultants may be members of the threat assessment unit or external experts. To be effective, a consultant should be knowledgeable in areas relevant to the case and be known and trusted by the investigators. For example, in a case where a subject has a history of diagnosed mental disorders and the primary investigator is unfamiliar with mental health language and concepts used in the records, an expert in psychology or psychiatry can provide invaluable insight and advice.

In addition to providing special expertise, consultants may notice and raise unanswered or unexplored questions in a case. Even proficient investigators are occasionally vulnerable to "missing the forest for the trees." A consultant, such as a fellow threat assessment specialist not involved with the case may offer a comment that can redirect or sharpen an ongoing investigation.

In the event of a bad outcome, use and documentation of consultant expertise may demonstrate the threat assessment team sought additional perspectives and ideas and did not suffer from "tunnel vision."

5.3.2.13. Closing the Case

The final task of threat assessment case management is closing the case. When a threat assessor determines the subject moved far enough away from possible violent action toward the target to no longer causing appreciable concern, the case can be considered for closing. At this time, it may be important to ask:

- What changed in the subject's life that appears to lessen the likelihood the subject is interested in or will attempt violent action toward the target?
- Which components of the case management plan seemed to affect the subject's thinking or capacity to initiate violent action and to what extent?
- What life circumstances might occur that would again put the subject at increased risk of contemplating, planning, or attempting violent action toward the original target or other potential targets?

- Are there supports in place or can be developed that will be known and available to the subject at a future time when the subject is again at risk of moving toward violent behavior?

While social commentators and analysts may debate the myriad reasons that lead to growing national concern about targeted violence, law enforcement and security organizations are increasingly being called on to examine individual situations and make judgments and determinations about the risks of violence a single person might present to an identifiable target.

In cases related to stalking behaviors, workplace violence, attacks on public officials and figures, and other situations where targeted violence is a possibility, comprehensive and carefully conducted threat assessment investigations can safeguard potential targets, deter potential attackers, and serve the public.

For further information about threat assessment, the publication titled *Protective Intelligence and Threat Assessment Investigations: A Guide for State and Local Law Enforcement Officials*[21] is available through the United States Secret Service website.

Appendix A, Case Study 4 provides practical examples of some of the issues discussed in this section.

5.4. Section 4: Employee Relations Considerations

Understanding employee relations issues that come into play in violent and potentially violent situations is important for all members of an agency's planning group. It helps in coordinating an effective response, in determining whether outside resources will be needed in certain situations, and in ensuring appropriate disciplinary actions are taken.

In many agencies, the employee relations staff coordinates the agency's workplace violence program. One reason is that most reported incidents will result in some type of disciplinary action. Another reason is that, since the goal of the workplace violence prevention effort is early and effective problem behavior management, reporting incidents to the employee relations office can result in swift disciplinary action that stops the unacceptable behavior before it can escalate. When another office, such as the security office, is responsible for coordinating the response effort, immediate involvement of the employee relations staff is usually necessary for an effective response.

This section will discuss

- Administrative options available in removing potentially dangerous employees from the worksite;
- Taking appropriate disciplinary action based on violent, threatening, harassing, and other disruptive behavior;
- Responding to an employee who raises a medical condition/disability as a defense against the misconduct;
- Ordering and offering psychiatric examinations;
- Assisting employees in applying for disability retirement; and
- Information on appeals of disciplinary actions.

5.4.1. Administrative Actions to Keep an Employee Away from the Worksite

In situations where a disruption occurred on the job or where there is a belief the potential for violence exists, a supervisor may need to bar an employee from the worksite to ensure the safety of employees while conducting further investigation and deciding on a course of action.

5.4.1.1. Immediate, Short-term Actions

- Place employee on excused absence (commonly known as administrative leave). Placing the employee in a paid, non-duty status is an immediate, temporary solution to the problem of an employee who should be kept away from the worksite.

  Some employees placed on excused absence consider this measure to be punitive. However, relevant statute and case law indicate that as long as the employee continues receiving pay and benefits just as if he or she were in a duty status, placing the employee in an excused absence status does not require the use of adverse action procedures set forth in 5 USC §7501 et. seq.

  Agencies should monitor the situation and move toward longer-term actions (as discussed below) when it is necessary, appropriate, or prudent to do so. Depending on the circumstances, it may also be a good idea to offer the employee the option to work at home while on excused leave.
- Detail employee to another position. This can be an effective way of getting an employee away from the worksite where he or she is causing other employees at the worksite to be disturbed. However,

this action will be useful only if there is another position where the employee can work safely and without disrupting other workers.

5.4.1.2. Long-Term Actions

Supervisors are sometimes faced with a situation where information is insufficient to determine if an employee poses a safety risk, actually committed a crime, or has a medical condition that might make disciplinary action inappropriate. To take an employee out of a paid duty status, an agency must use adverse action procedures that require a 30-day paid status during the advance notice of the adverse action. Included below are the two types of actions that place an employee in non-duty status.

- **Indefinite suspension**. An indefinite suspension is an adverse action that takes an employee off duty until the completion of some ongoing inquiry, such as an agency investigation into allegations of misconduct. Agencies usually propose indefinite suspensions when they will need more than 30 days to await the results of an investigation, await the completion of a criminal proceeding, or make a determination on the employee's medical condition. Indefinite suspensions are 5 CFR § 752 adverse actions requiring a 30-day notice period with pay. This means that 30 days after an indefinite suspension is proposed the employee will no longer be in a pay status until the completion of the investigation, completion of the criminal proceeding, or determination of the employee's medical condition.
- **Indefinite enforced leave.** The procedure for indefinite enforced leave is the same as for an indefinite suspension—§ 752 adverse action procedures. It involves making the employee use his or her own sick or annual leave (after the 30-day notice period with pay) pending the outcome of an inquiry.

5.4.2. Disciplinary Actions

Where the supervisor possesses the relevant information regarding violent, harassing, threatening, and other disruptive behavior, the supervisor must determine the appropriate disciplinary action.

Disciplining an employee for abusive, threatening, or violent behavior serves two purposes. For the abusive or violent employee, the disciplinary action should serve as an appropriate penalty for past conduct and a deterrent against future offenses. For the rest of the work force, it should serve to reaffirm the employer's commitment to a workplace free from threats and violence and reinforce employees' confidence that thei r safety is protected by strong but fair measures. To achieve those goals, penalties and the disci pl i nary process must be—and must be seen to be—proportionate, consistent, reasonable, and fair.

The selection of an appropriate charge and related penalty should be discussed with the employee relations staff and the OGC where appropriate. Some disci pl i nary actions are:

- **Reprimand, warning, short suspension, and alternative discipline**. These lesser disciplinary actions can be used in cases where the misconduct is not serious and progressive discipline may correct the problem behavior. These lesser disciplinary actions are an excel lent means of dealing with problem behavior early in the process. They involve considerably fewer procedures than the adverse actions l isted immediately below.
- **Removal, reduction-in grade, and suspension for more than 14 days**. Law and regulations[22] provide that an agency may take an adverse action against an employee only for such cause as will promote the efficiency of the service. A Federal employee against whom an adverse action is proposed is entitled to a 30-day advance written notice. A 7-day notice period instead of the usual 30 days is permitted "when the agency has reasonable cause to believe that the employee has committed a cri me for which a sentence of imprisonment may be imposed."[23]

In either case, the agency must give the reasons for the proposed action i n the written notice and provide the employee an opportunity to respond. The agency must consider the employee's response and notify the employee when a decision has been made. If the agency's final decision is to take the proposed action, the employee must be advised of the appeal rights to which he or she is entitled and the ti me limits that apply to those appeal rights.

5.4.3. Disabilities as a Defense against Alleged Misconduct

The Equal Employment Opportunity Commission (EEOC) issued important guidance specifically addressing potentially violent misconduct by employees with disabilities. Although this guidance deals specifically with psychiatric disabilities, it applies generally to other disabling medical conditions. It advises that an agency may discipline an employee with a disability who violated a job-related rule (written or unwritten) and consistent with business necessity, even if the misconduct is the result of the disability, as long as the agency would impose the same discipline on an employee without a disability. The guidance specifically states that nothing in the Rehabilitation Act prevents an employer from maintaining a workplace free of violence or threats of violence.

The guidance specifically states reasonable accommodation is always prospective. Thus, an agency is never required to excuse past misconduct as a reasonable accommodation. A reasonable accommodation is a change to the workplace that helps an employee perform his or her job and may be required, along with discipline, when the discipline is less than removal.

For a detailed discussion of these points, see *EEOC Enforcement Guidance on the Americans with Disabilities Act and Psychiatric Disabilities*, EEOC number 915.002, 3-25-97[24]. Interpretation of the Rehabilitation Act is complex, and any specific questions should be discussed with your OGC.

5.4.4. Ordering and Offering Psychiatric Examinations

Supervisors should gain a better understanding of their rights (and limitations) regarding psychiatric examinations for employees. There are some absolute prohibitions in Federal personnel regulations regarding what medical information a supervisor can demand from an employee and every supervisor should learn what can be ordered and what can be offered. Discuss specific questions with your OGC. However, below is some basic information on psychiatric examinations.

5.4.4.1. Ordering a Psychiatric Examination

Under 5 CFR § 339, an agency may order a psychiatric examination, or psychological assessment, under very rare circumstances.[25] The only time an employee can be ordered to undergo a psychiatric examination is:

- If he or she occupies a position requiring specific medical standards and the results of a current general medical exam the agency has the authority to order show no physical basis to explain actions or behavior that may affect the safe and efficient performance of the individual or others; or
- If a psychiatric examination is specifically required by medical standards or a medical evaluation program.

5.4.4.2. Offering a Psychiatric Examination

Under 5 CFR § 339, an agency may offer a psychiatric evaluation or psychological assessment (or it may ask the employee to submit medical documentation) in any situation where it is in the interest of the Government to obtain information relevant to an individual's ability to perform safely and efficiently, or when the employee has requested, for medical reasons relating to a psychiatric condition, a change in duty status, working conditions, or any other benefit or reasonable accommodation. If the employee decides not to be examined or to submit medical documentation, the agency should act on the basis of the information available.

5.4.5. Disability Retirement

Supervisors should also gain a better understanding of their rights and limitations regarding assisting employees with disability retirement applications. The restrictions on filing a disability retirement on behalf of an employee are rigorous, so supervisors should understand their role in encouraging and assisting employees who wish to seek disability retirement. Below is some basic information on disability retirement.

Employees with medical disabilities may be eligible for disability retirement if their medical condition warrants it and if they have the requisite years of Federal service to qualify. In considering applications for disability retirement from employees, the OPM focuses on the extent of the employee's incapacitation and ability to perform his or her assigned duties. OPM makes every effort to expedite any applications where the employee's illness is in an advanced stage.

It is important to note that OPM's regulations[26] specifically provide that an individual's application for disability retirement does not stop or stay an agency's taking and effecting an adverse action. An agency should continue to process an adverse action even while informing the employee of his or her ability to file an application for disability retirement, or informing family members they can apply on behalf of the employee.

5.4.5.1. Assisting Employees in Applying for Disability Retirement

The agency can and should counsel the employee any time it believes a medical condition is causing a service deficiency and the employee is otherwise eligible for disability retirement. This does not mean the agency has a specific number of documents in hand to show the employee is medically incapacitated. It only means disability retirement is being presented as an option to the employee.

The agency cannot force the employee to file an application for disability retirement, despite its belief it is in his or her best interest. If the agency believes the employee does not understand the consequences of his or her choice not to do so, the next paragraph explains agency-filed applications for disability retirement.

5.4.5.2. Agency-filed Application for Disability Retirement

The conditions for filing an application for disability retirement on behalf of an employee are strictly limited. OPM set out five conditions that must be met before an agency can file on an employee's behalf.[27] If the following five conditions are met, the agency must file on the employee's behalf.

- The agency has issued a decision to remove the employee;
- The agency concludes, after review of medical documentation, the cause of the unacceptable performance, conduct, or leave problems is due to the disease or injury;
- The employee is institutionalized, or based on the agency's review of medical and other information, it concludes that the employee is incapable of making a decision to file on his or her own behalf;
- The employee has no representative or guardian with the authority to file on his or her behalf; and
- The employee has no immediate family member (spouse, parent, or adult child) who is willing to file on his or her behalf.

5.4.6. Appeals of a Disciplinary Action

Once a disciplinary action is taken by an agency, the employee involved has options regarding his or her appeal (or challenge) to the agency's final decision. Various avenues of redress may be available to an employee including the agency's administrative or negotiated grievance system, EEOC, or the MSPB. Employees covered by a bargaining unit often turn to the union for guidance on their appeal rights.

Numerous holdings by third parties uphold agencies' rights to discipline employees who have threatened, intimidated, or physically injured their supervisors or coworkers, or otherwise caused a disruption in the workplace. However, since case law relating to disciplinary actions is constantly evolving, agency officials should always consult their employee/labor relations specialists and Office of the General Counsel when considering disciplinary actions.

Appendix A, Case Studies 3, 5, 10, and 12 provide practical examples of some of the issues discussed in this section.

5.5. Section 5: Employee Assistance Program Considerations

Employee Assistance Program (EAP) participation can be important to the success of an agency's workplace violence program. The EAP's role generally begins with participation on the agency planning group where decisions are made about the role the EAP will play in the workplace violence program. EAPs usually play an active role in early prevention efforts, sometimes participate on the incident response team, and generally assist with organizational recovery after an incident of workplace violence has occurred. This section will provide an overview of the EAP and then discuss considerations specific to workplace violence.

5.5.1. Overview of the Employee Assistance Program

Every Federal agency has an EAP that provides short-term counseling and referral services to its employees at no cost. These programs are staffed by professional counselors who are available to discuss problems that can adversely affect job performance, conduct, and reliability. EAPs are required to help employees deal with alcoholism or drug abuse problems, and most programs also help employees with other problems such as marital or financial problems. EAP counselors often refer employees to other professional services and resources within the community for further information, assistance, or long-term counseling.

EAPs differ from agency to agency in their structure and scope of services. Some are in-house programs, staffed by employees of the agency. Others are contracted or operated through an interagency agreement with the Department of Health and Human Services' (HHS) Division of Federal Occupational Health. Among contracted programs, services differ, depending on the terms of the contract and the relationship between the agency and the contractor.

Confidentiality is an important issue for EAPs. Employees who seek EAP services are afforded considerable privacy by laws, policies, and the professional ethics of EAP professionals. It is common practice for EAPs to inform employees in writing about the limits of confidentiality on their first visit.

Agency planning group members should familiarize themselves with the structure, scope, and special considerations of their agency's EAP. As the planning group explores the range of services provided, it may identify needs for expanding the program's existing array of services. EAP professionals should advise the agency planning group on the relevant laws, policies, and professional ethical constraints under which they operate, including the Privacy Act provisions of 5 USC §552a and the HHS Alcohol and Drug Patient Confidentiality Regulation provisions of 42 CFR § 2. This will allow cooperative arrangements to be worked out for an appropriate EAP role.

5.5.2. The Employee Assistance Program's Role in Dealing with Workplace Violence

5.5.2.1. Supportive Resources and Care

Immediately after a violent incident, the main priority is to provide safety, security, and necessary medical attention by the appropriate security, law enforcement, and emergency medical response personnel. These designated personnel will secure the work area and assess the possibility of any continued threat. It is also important to account for all building occupants (employees, visitors, contractors, service providers, etc.), and it is vital they be able to contact family, friends, and significant others as soon as possible.

Victims, intended victims, bystanders, and coworkers may all experience both short- and long-term psychological distress as the result of a workplace violence incident. Exposure to traumatic events often leads to a range of strong emotional and physical responses, so it is important to engage and use available resources to evaluate at-risk individuals who may be in need of treatment. Agencies will likely have a variety of options for evaluating and providing support for those who may be affected. Some of those options may include:

- EAPs;
- Private practice mental health services;
- Community mental health resources;
- Educational sessions on stress responses, coping, and available services;
- Facilitating existing support networks; and
- Providing opportunities for private, individual discussions.

EAP staff members generally assist in policy and strategy development and help determine the EAP's role on the agency's workplace violence incident response team. EAPs bring a special expertise to the planning process. They are in an optimal position to assist with many of the activities conducted by the planning group.

5.5.2.2. Role in Early Prevention Efforts

- **Promotion of the EAP**. The effectiveness of a workplace violence program is greatly enhanced in an organization with an active, well-known EAP presence. Agencies with active programs promote the EAP by issuing periodic statements from top management endorsing the program and reminding employees of the services offered by the EAP, having counselors attend staff meetings to familiarize agency employees with the counselors, and having counselors give special briefings and seminars for managers, employees, and union stewards.
- **Information dissemination**. EAPs often provide booklets, pamphlets, and lending libraries of books and videos about such topics as domestic violence, stress reduction, and dealing with angry customers.
- **Early involvement in organizational change.** When an agency is facing reorganization, restructuring, or other organizational change that may have a negative effect on employees, the EAP can help, through individual or group sessions, keep information flowing, keep feelings under control, prevent potential outbursts, provide constructive outlets for feelings, and help employees plan for the future.
- **Employee and supervisory training.** Much of the employee training described in Chapter 4, Section 3 is conducted by EAP staff. For example, counselors can train employees on such topics as dealing with angry coworkers and customers, conflict resolution, and communications skills. Since EAP staff understands how important it is that supervisors (and coworkers) refrain from diagnosing an employee's problem, they are in an excellent position to explain the delicate balance between identifying problem behavior early on and labeling an individual as potentially violent. EAP counselors can train supervisors to deal with problems as soon as they surface without diagnosing the employee's problem.

5.5.2.3. Participation on an Incident Response Team

Since every reported incident of workplace violence is different and every agency is structured differently, EAP participation on an incident response team will depend on many factors. Issues need to be clarified ahead of time to avoid misunderstanding and conflict. Team members need to understand that if a case is being discussed and the counselor says, "Sorry, I can't help you with this one," they should neither expect an explanation nor assume the counselor is being uncooperative. Advance planning can help to identify ways of coping with these types of issues. If, for example, the EAP is large enough, then different staff members may play different roles or the staff may be able to identify other professionals who can be brought in to ensure all needs are addressed. Working with other members of the planning group and the incident response team in advance can clarify the EAP's role when an incident arises.

5.5.2.4. Consultation with Supervisor when an Incident is Reported

Depending on the type of incident reported, it is often important for a counselor, along with an employee relations specialist and security officer, to be part of the incident response team that consults with the manager. In some situations, such as potential suicides, the EAP can play a major role. In other situations, such as dealing with an employee who frightens coworkers, but who has not actually done or said anything warranting discipline, the EAP can assist other team members in working with the supervisor to plan an effective response.

5.5.2.5. Response/Intervention

The counselor can help with conflict resolution in situations eported early enough for such an intervention. The counselor can work with the victim by giving advice and guidance, or with the perpetrator by helping to diffuse the anger/hostility that could lead to violence. The counselor can help clarify options and procedures for situations where substance abuse or mental illness seems to be a factor. For example, states differ in their laws regarding civil commitment for psychiatric treatment. The counselor can explain to other team members the EAP role in such a situation and can coordinate with other community resources to develop contingency plans for various emergency situations. These and other examples are illustrated in the case studies in Appendix A.

5.5.2.6. Follow-up to a Violent Incident

Many EAPs are prepared to respond promptly to a variety of needs that may exist after a violent incident. Prompt individual interventions with employees who had particularly stressful experiences are sometimes necessary. Debriefing sessions for groups are often conducted two or three days after the incident. The EAP can also act as consultants to management in helping the organization to recover.

5.5.2.7. Individual Interventions

Though most employees will need only brief intervention, provision should be made for the few who may need longer-term professional assistance. Strategies for identifying these employees and guiding them as smoothly as possible from emergency-centered interventions to more extensive mental health care should be included in the planning.

The EAP may approach these responsibilities in different ways, depending on the size and experience of its staff. In some cases, internal EAP resources may be sufficient, but in others, additional staffing will be necessary. EAP staff members who do not have expertise in traumatic incident counseling may wish to develop in-house expertise or keep close at hand the phone numbers of resources to contact should an incident occur.

Potential sources of additional help, for example, private contractors, community mental health resources, and university or medical school programs, might be explored.

5.5.2.8. Critical Incident Stress Debriefings

Many EAPs are trained to participate on Critical Incident Stress Debriefings (CISD) teams. See discussion of the CISD process in Chapter 5, Section 5.7.

5.5.2.9. Acting as Consultants to Management

Since management bears the brunt of responsibility after a violent incident and can find itself dealing with unfamiliar challenges under high stress, the EAP can be very helpful in facilitating an optimal response. It can provide managers with information on traumatic events and can assist them in analyzing the situation and developing strategies for the organization's recovery. An effective EAP needs to be familiar not only with post-disaster mental health care, but also with management practices facilitating recovery and with other resources that may need to be mobilized.

In thinking about an organization's recovery, there is a temptation to focus narrowly on care-giving responses such as debriefings and counseling discussed above. Essential as these services are, they are only part of the picture. The way the manager conveys information, schedules responsibilities, sets priorities, and monitors employee performance after a violent incident can play a vital role in helping or hindering recovery. Some EAPs are trained to provide this type of consultation. Agencies will find *A Manager's Handbook: Handling Traumatic Events* helpful in this regard. See Section 7 in this chapter for further information on organizational recovery and Appendix A for information on obtaining a copy of the *Manager's Handbook*.

5.5.3. Other EAP Considerations for the Agency Planning Group

5.5.3.1. Should the EAP Take the Incident Report?

Most agencies do not use the EAP as the office responsible for taking incident reports on workplace violence. Following are some of the reasons cited by agencies.

Because confidentiality requirements prohibit EAP counselors from disclosing information, putting a counselor in the position of informing the other members of the intervention team about the report could lead to serious misunderstandings among agency employees and harm the credibility of the EAP. It sometimes takes years to build the EAP into a viable program trusted by employees to keep any contacts confidential and the dual role could diminish this viability.

In addition, the incident reports could get confused with EAP records covered by the agency's internal system of records for its EAP under the Privacy Act. Records filed and retrieved by name or other personal identifier are subject to the Privacy Act provisions of 5 USC §552a. Since each agency's system of records is different, it is a good idea to check with the agency's Privacy Act Officer regarding the systems notice for the agency's EAP. The systems notice covers who can gain access to the records and how amendments are made to the records.

Many times the EAP counselor will be the person who first hears about an incident involving threatening behavior, even though the agency's reporting system provides for another office to take incident reports. Managers and employees often feel comfortable telling the counselor about a situation that frightens them. The agency's planning group should decide ahead of time the types of reports the counselors should handle alone and the types that should be reported to the other team members, always making sure each member of the team understands the confidentiality requirements of the EAP.

Please refer to the following OPM website for further information on this section: http://www.opm.gov /Employment_and_Benefits/WorkLife/Official Documents/HandbooksGuides/Confi dentiality_EAP/index.asp.

5.5.3.2. Should the EAP be the First to Intervene?

Agencies who have had experience with the EAP as the first intervener in workplace violence situations report they do not recommend this approach for the following reasons:

- Issues of confidentiality cause numerous conflicts for the counselors; and
- It could lead to a perception of treating perpetrators of workplace violence as victims needing counseling rather than as perpetrators needing discipline.

Therefore, the agency planning group should ensure procedures developed ahead of time allow for flexibility and do not require counselors to be the first interveners in situations where this would be inappropriate.

5.5.3.3. Should the EAP Perform Psychological Exams?

Organizations with experience in offering psychological or psychiatric examinations usually recommend that these not be performed by the EAP staff. The process of conducting examinations is not only time consuming and highly specialized, but fits poorly with other EAP responsibilities. Thus, most agencies find it preferable, if offering such an examination, to have it done by an "outsider" such as an external contractor. Some agencies have professional mental health staffs in addition to the EAP and utilize them for this type of evaluation. The EAP can then take the role of teacher and facilitator, helping everyone involved to understand the report of the examination and put its recommendations into practice.

Appendix A, Case Studies 1, 2, 6, 9, 11, 13, 14, and 16 provide practical examples of some of the issues discussed in this section.

5.6. Section 6: Workplace Security

Law enforcement, security officers, and the designated Facility Security Committee (FSC) members should be involved in all stages of the planning process in an effective workplace violence prevention program. They can play an active role in prevention, intervention, and response to threatening situations, in addition to their traditional role of responding to actual incidents of physical violence. This section will provide general ideas and considerations that can help the agency planning group gain a greater understanding of the ISC's Facility Security Level (FSL) determination process and an understanding of some of the law enforcement/security issues such as jurisdiction. It is also intended to help those Federal offices that do not have in-house security or law enforcement identify the appropriate organizations that can assist them. To request access to the ISC documents, please contact the ISC at ISCAccess@dhs.gov.

5.6.1. Making the Facility Security Level Determination

The initial FSL determination is the first step in developing the highest achievable security countermeasures for a facility. The determination should be made early enough in the space acquisition process to allow for the implementation of required countermeasures or reconsideration of the acquisition caused by an inability to meet minimum physical security requirements.

Risk assessments will be conducted at least every five years for Level I and Level II facilities and at least every three years for Level III, Level IV, and Level V facilities. The FSL will be reviewed and adjusted, if necessary, as part of each initial and recurring risk assessment.

The responsibility for making the final FSL determination rests with the tenant(s), who must determine the risk management strategy to pursue in order to reduce the risk.

For single-tenant Government-owned or –leased facilities, a representative of the tenant agency will make the FSL determination, in consultation with the owning or leasing department or agency and the security organization(s) responsible for the facility.

In multi-tenant Government-owned or –leased facilities, the designated official, in coordination with a representative of each Federal tenant (i.e., the FSC), will make the FSL determination in consultation with the owning/leasing department or agency and the security organization(s) responsible for the facility.

When the security organization(s) and the owner/leasing authority do not agree with the tenant agency representative or designated official with regard to the FSL determination, the ISC as the representative of the Secretary of Homeland Security will facilitate the final determination.

The FSL determination should be documented, signed, and retained by all parties to the decision. Once the FSL for the facility is determined, protective countermeasures appropriate for the facility as prescribed by ISC standards are to be taken.

5.6.2. Law Enforcement and Security Assistance

During the planning phase, law enforcement/security officers can:

- Identify situations they can address;
- Identify when and how they should be notified of an incident;
- Indicate whether their officers have arrest authority;
- Identify jurisdictional restrictions and alternative law enforcement agencies that may assist;
- Identify threat assessment personnel who partner with the agency to protect threatened
- employees;
- Advise on what evidence is necessary and how it can be collected or recorded;
- Utilize collected or recorded evidence to decide the appropriate level of action to take;
- Explain anti-stalking laws applicable in the agency's jurisdiction;
- Explain when and how to obtain restraining orders;
- Suggest security measures to be taken for specific situations; and
- Arrange for supervisor/employee briefings or training on workplace violence issues such as:
    - Personal safety and security measures;
    - Types of incidents to report to law enforcement/security;
    - Types of measures law enforcement/security may take to protect employees during an incident;
    - Suggestions on how to react to an armed attacker;
    - Suggestions for dealing with angry customers or clients;
    - Suspicious packages;
    - Bomb threats;
    - Hostage situations; and
    - Telephone harassment and threats.

When potentially violent situations arise, law enforcement/security officers can work with the incident response team to:

- Provide an assessment of the information available;
- Determine whether law enforcement intervention is immediately necessary;
- Identify what plan of action they deem appropriate; and
- Determine who will gather what types of evidence.

5.6.3. Physical Security Measures

Planning groups should review security measures and procedures as well as make recommendations for modifications and improvements. Many Federal agencies have numerous security measures in place that can reduce the risk of workplace violence. These include:

- Closed circuit cameras;
- Silent alarms;
- Metal detectors;
- Two-way mirrors;
- Electronic access systems;
- Barriers to prevent cars from driving too close to the building;
- Emergency internal code words;
- Extra lighting in the parking lots; and
- Escorts to and from parking lots after dark.

The information in the following section regarding physical security has been provided by the Department of Homeland Security's (DHS) Federal Protective Service (FPS).

5.6.4. Physical Security in GSA Owned or Leased Buildings

There are more than 900,000 employees working in approximately 9,000 GSA owned or leased Federal buildings. DHS is the agency responsible for ensuring the safety and security of people while on Federal property owned or leased by GSA. This section contains recommendations and requirements for agencies in GSA controlled or leased space.

5.6.4.1. Regulations

Federal Property Management Regulations 41 CFR § 101-20 and EO12656 specifically require GSA to provide standard protection services by coordinating an OEP that is a short-term emergency response program establishing procedures for safeguarding lives and property during emergencies.

5.6.4.2. U.S. General Services Administration Designated Official

Each GSA-owned or -leased facility has a designated official. A designated official is either the highest ranking official of the primary occupant agency of a Federal facility or a designee selected by mutual agreement of occupant agency officials. The designated official is responsible for developing, implementing, and maintaining an Occupant Emergency Plan that consists of procedures developed to protect life and property in specific Federal-occupied space under stipulated emergency conditions. In addition, the designated official's responsibilities include establishing, staffing, and training an Occupant Emergency Organization, comprised of agency employees designated to perform the requirements established by the OEP.

According to the regulations, the GSA must assist in the establishment and maintenance of such plans and organizations. All agencies occupying a facility must fully cooperate with the designated official in the implementation of the emergency plans and the staffing of the emergency organization. GSA must:

- Provide emergency program policy guidance;
- Review plans and organizations annually;
- Assist in training of personnel; and
- Ensure proper administration of Occupant Emergency Programs.

In leased space, GSA will solicit the assistance of the lessor and in the establishment and implementation of plans.

The regulation states decisions to activate the Occupant Emergency Organization shall be made by the designated official or by the designated alternate official. Decisions to activate shall be based upon the best available information, including an understanding of local tensions, the sensitivity of target agencies, and previous experience with similar situations. Advice shall be solicited from the GSA buildings manager, the appropriate FPS official, and from Federal, state, and local law enforcement agencies.

5.6.5. Physical Security Survey

A major goal of FPS, when they have jurisdiction, is to provide better protection for Federal employees and visitors by pinpointing high-risk areas in Federal buildings. This is accomplished through a Physical Security Survey conducted by a security specialist. The survey is a comprehensive, detailed, technical on-site inspection and analysis of the current security and physical protection conditions.

If the agency does not have current security procedures in place, the head of the agency may ask the agency's security office (if a non-FPS facility) or a regional FPS office to conduct a physical security survey in the effort to ensure that employees are working in a safe and secure environment. There is a listing of FPS offices at the end of this section.

The following are some examples provided by the FPS of ways to improve office and/or building security:

- Post a security guard at the main building entrance or at entrances to specific offices;
- Install a metal detector or closed-circuit television camera or other device;
- Issue all employees photo identification cards;
- Assign temporary passes to visitors;
- Contract guards should be required to call Federal offices to confirm an appointment as necessary;
- Request an escort for all visitors: customers, relatives, or friends;
- Brief employees on an action plan should a threatening or violent incident occur;
- Establish code words to alert coworkers and supervisors that immediate help is needed; and
- Install silent, concealed alarms at reception desks.

The following are some examples provided by FPS of options to improve security in the event of a threatening or violent individual:

- Ensure officers or guards have a clear view of the customer service area at all times;
- Arrange furniture and partitions so front-line employees are surrounded by a barrier;
- Provide an under-the-counter duress alarm system to signal a supervisor or security officer;
- Establish an area in the office for employees and/or customers to escape;
- Provide an access-control combination lock on access doors; and

- Mount closed circuit television cameras from a central security office for the building.

Additional resources regarding options to improve employee security can be found in the Resources portion of this document.

Note: Any measure not covered under the standard security agreement with FPS may have a fee associated with that service.

5.6.6. Computer Security

Agency planning groups should address ways to safeguard computer systems. There are cases where employees sabotaged computer equipment, computer systems, and computer records. Therefore, whenever a threat of sabotage is suspected, procedures should be initiated to prevent the person from having access to the facility's computer system.

It is important to act quickly whenever there is reason to believe an employee or former employee may commit such an act. It is standard practice to collect identification cards, building passes, keys, and parking passes when employees leave their jobs; however, blocking access to computer systems or networks is sometimes overlooked.

When terminating employees, some agencies bar the individual from the premises and eradicate their passwords to computer systems that are accessible from outside the premises.

"The agency planning group, as part of the response plan, should talk to the information/computer security officer or computer system administrators to determine the vulnerability of the computer networks and the procedures that need to be implemented to lock individuals out of these systems."

Identifying all access to information is sometimes difficult to determine; often, it is not readily available in one central place. For example, information technology administrators may know who has access to various computer systems, and the facilities manager may know who has access to the computer systems that control the building's heating, air-conditioning, and other support functions for the facility. The agency planning group, as part of the response plan, should talk to the information/computer security officer or computer system administrators to determine the vulnerability of the computer networks and the procedures that need to be implemented to lock individuals out of these systems.

5.6.7. Examples of Handouts

The following pages contain examples of handouts developed by FPS that can be used by or adapted for your agency. In addition, a listing of the FPS regional offices is provided at the end of this section. The regional offices may be contacted for additional brochures and literature on office safety and security. Printer-friendly versions of the materials are also available.

5.6.7.1. Desk Card

Figure 1 summarizes the actions you should or should not take in a hostile or threatening situation. Print out and detach the card, fold the card into a "tent," and tape the ends together underneath so that the card will stand up on your desk with the text facing you. Review the card often. If you are confronted by an angry, hostile, or threatening customer or co-worker, you will know what you should do. Everyone in your office, including supervisors and managers, should follow these same procedures.

Copies can be made of this card so that all employees have their own card.

Coping with Threats and Violence

For an angry or hostile customer or co-worker:

- Stay calm and listen attentively
- Maintain eye contact
- Be courteous and patient
- Keep the situationin your control

For a person shouting, swearing, and threatening:

- Signal a co-worker or a supervisor that you need help
- Use a duress alarm system or prearranged code words
- Do not make any calls yourself
- Have someone call the FPS, contract guard, or local police

For someone threatening you with a gun, knife, or other weapon

- Stay calm and quietly signal for help
- Use a duress alarm or code word
- Maintain eye contact
- Stall for time
- Keep talking, but follow instructions from the person who has the weapon
- Never try to grab a weapon
- Watch for a safe chance to escape to a safe area

Figure 1. Sample Reference Card for Coping with Threats and Violence (Source: Federal Protective Service and U.S. General Services Administration, 1998).

5.6.7.2. Reference Card

Figure 2, Telephone Threats, lists guidance for how to approach a threatening phone call. Everyone in your office, including supervisors and managers, should follow these same procedures. Make copies of the card if you need to so everyone will have his or her own card.

Telephone Threats

- Keep calm
- Keep talking
- Don't hang up
- Signal a co-working to get on an extension
- Ask the caller to repeat the message and write it down
- Repeat questions if necessary
- For a bomb threat, ask for the location of the bomb and detonation time
- Listen for background noises and write down a description
- Note the caller's gender, voice pitch, accent, additional sounds
- Try to get the person's name, exact location, and telephone number
- Signal a co-worker to immediately call the FPS, contract guard, or the localpolice
- Notify your immediate supervisor

Figure 2. Sample Reference Card for Coping with Telephone Threats (Source: Federal Protective Service and U.S. General Services Administration, 1998).

5.6.7.3. Emergency Phone Numbers

Figure 3, Emergency Telephone Numbers, provides a sample template for having all the emergency numbers for our building in one place. Carefully tear out the "Emergency Phone Numbers" card. Tape this card on your desk by your phone.

Emergency Telephone Numbers
Federal Protective Service (FPS): ______________________
Building Security: ______________________________
Local Police/Sheriff: ____________________________

Source: Federal Protective Service and U.S. General Services Administration, 1998.

Figure 3. Sample Emergency Phone Card for Emergency Telephone Numbers.

5.6.8. Federal Protective Service Offices

For more information on coping with threats and violence in Federal offices, other crime prevention, security surveys, and protection assistance, write or call your nearest FPS, Public Buildings Service, U.S. Department of Homeland Security at one of these regional addresses:

<table>
<tr><td>Washington, DC Metropolitan Area
Southeast Federal Center
3rd & M Streets S. E.
Washington, DC 20407-0001
(202) 690-9632</td><td>Crime Prevention Program
18th & F St., NW
Washington, DC 20405-0002
(202) 501-0907</td></tr>
<tr><td colspan="2" align="center">U.S. Office of Personnel Management
1900 E Street, NW
Washington, DC 20415
(202) 606-1800 | TTY (202) 606-2532</td></tr>
<tr><td>Region I
Connecticut, Maine, Massachusetts, New Hampshire, Vermont, Rhode Island
10 Causeway Street, Room 108
Boston, MA 02222-1098 (617) 565-5776</td><td>Region II
New York, New Jersey, Puerto Rico, U. S. Virgin Islands
26 Federal Plaza
New York, NY 10278-0013
(212) 264-4255</td></tr>
<tr><td>Region III
Delaware, Maryland and Virginia, Pennsylvania, West Virginia
100 Penn Square, East
Philadelphia, PA 19107-3396
(215) 656-6043</td><td>Region IV
Alabama, Florida, Georgia, Kentucky, Mississippi, North Carolina, South Carolina, Tennessee
401 West Peachtree Street, NW
Atlanta, GA 30365-2550 (404) 331-5132</td></tr>
<tr><td>Region V
Illinois, Indiana, Michigan, Minnesota, Ohio, Wisconsin
230 South Dearborn Street Chicago, IL 60604-1503
(312) 353-1496</td><td>Region VI
Arkansas, Louisiana, New Mexico, Oklahoma, Texas
819 Taylor Street
Fort Worth, TX, 76102-6105
(817) 334-3559</td></tr>
</table>

(Continued)

Region VII *Iowa, Kansas, Missouri, Nebraska* 1500 Bannister Road Kansas City, MO 64131-3088 (816) 926-7025	Region VIII *Colorado, Montana, North Dakota, South Dakota, Utah, Wyoming* Building 41, Denver Federal Center Denver, CO 80225-0546 (303) 236-5869
Region IX *Arizona, California, Hawaii, Nevada, Guam, U. S. Trust Territory of the Pacific* 450 Golden Gate Avenue San Francisco, CA 94102-3400 (415) 522-3440	**Region X** *Alaska, Idaho, Oregon, Washington* 400 15th Street, SW Auburn, WA 98001-6599 (206) 931-7529

5.7. Section 7: Organizational Recovery Post-Incident

Despite the best-laid plans of any Federal agency, violence in the workplace can and does happen. Agencies should develop both policies and procedures designed to head off these occurrences as well as preparations to deal with the aftermath of such incidents. Quite often, management focuses on continuity of operations; however, mitigating the impact such incidents have on office personnel is equally important. This section provides information designed to assist management with helping an organization to recover after an incident of workplace violence.

5.7.1. Management Steps to Help an Organization Recover

Provided below are several initial steps management can take when an incident of workplace violence occurs.

5.7.1.1. Ensure a Management Presence at the Work Site

Managers need to spend ample time with their employees. Employees need to be reassured of their concern, and they need to be able to ask questions. Senior management should ensure immediate supervisors are supported in this role, relieved of unnecessary duties, and not pulled away from their subordinates to write lengthy reports or prepare elaborate briefings.

5.7.1.2. Share Information with Employees

It is important for managers to share information with the rest of the workplace community as rapidly and honestly as possible, so false reports and irrational fears do not spread and make the situation worse. Employees will have many questions, and they need the answers, often more than once, if they are to resolve the experience for themselves. Information will develop over time; therefore, information strategies need to be simple and fluid. A notice board at the elevator or a recorded message on a "hotline" number may suffice for the basics, and organizations might also consider establishing a user-friendly system for individual questions.

5.7.1.3. Include Union Leadership

Union representatives can help in reassuring employees after an incident and in getting information to employees.

5.7.1.4. Bring in Crisis Response Professionals

Prior to an incident, the planning group should identify trained mental health professionals in the agency's EAP or the community who would be available to respond in the event of an incident. Some organizations may wish to develop their own in-house capacity to deliver best practices in psychological aspects of incident response, since these may not be available locally. Psychological service can offer victims and their coworkers comfort, information, support, and help with practical needs. It can also spot those who appear most troubled by the event and may need more intensive psychological attention in the future.

When an incident occurs, involve emergency mental health consultants as soon as possible. They will generally meet with management first, working down the chain, and then with employees. Based on the findings, consultants will offer various services. Examples of possible services include the following:

- **Support Informal Debriefing:** The formal debriefing does not end the recovery process. Provide opportunities for employees to talk informally with one another when they feel a need to discuss the experience. A comfortable break area and flexibility about break times may be all that is needed.
- **Support Care giving within Work Groups:** Keep work units together as much as possible, and try not to isolate employees from

their normal support groups at work. Show respect and support for employees' efforts to care for one another.

- **Handle Critical Sites with Care:** Initially, the site of a violent incident will be secured as a crime scene. After the authorities clear the scene and collect necessary information, management needs to be sensitive to a number of issues. It is helpful if employees don't have to come back to work and face painful reminders such as blood stains or broken furniture. But on the other hand, the area should not be so "sanitized" that it gives the appearance that management is pretending nothing happened. If someone has died, that person's work area will be a focus of grieving and it needs to be respected as such.
- **Buffer Those Affected from Post-Event Stresses:** Effective coordination with the media and timely dissemination of information can help reduce media pressure on those who are the most vulnerable. Questions from the news media relating to incidents of workplace violence should be forwarded to the appropriate public affairs staff for the agency. Assistance with benefits and other administrative issues can reduce the burden on victims and families.
- **Help Employees Face Feared Places or Activities:** Returning soon to a feared site, if only briefly, can help prevent lasting effects such as phobic responses. Having a friend or loved one along or being supported by close work associates may make the first step much easier.
- **Remember the Healing Value of Routine:** Getting back to a regular routine can be reassuring, and a sense of having a mission to perform at work can help the group recover its morale. The return to work must be managed in a way that conveys appropriate respect for the deceased, the injured, and the traumatized.
- **Follow-Up with Those Exposed to Extreme Stressors:** Some individuals may be especially at risk for continuing emotional problems due to the nature of their exposure (e.g., survivor of a severe physical assault; sexual assault survivor). Follow-up with these individuals can facilitate monitoring of continuing stress reactions and enable increase in intensity of services as needed.

5.7.2. The Critical Incident Stress Management Process

Following traumatic events in the workplace, employees often experience short-term behavioral and mood adjustment problems or symptoms of post-traumatic stress disorder. Agency managers should address these issues by advising all employees to access the agency's EAP service to assist with any strong negative emotions, anger, sleep problems, or other normal reactions to the abnormal event. In addition, most Federal employees will have mental health services available through their Federal health insurance benefits. Seeking help for adjustment problems should be characterized by managers in a normalizing manner, but should not be pushed or mandated. Not all EAP services have immediately accessible emergency response capability. It is important to determine this capacity exists, EAP providers have been trained, and the planned response is consistent with best response practices.

Generally, immediate behavioral health responses should not be attempted except by a mental health professional well-versed in the risks and benefits of "psychological first aid" and crisis counseling methods. In more recent years, research studies of the most commonly used formal crisis intervention process, stress debriefing, consistently show that stress debriefing does not prevent development of post-traumatic stress disorder or depression, and some investigators found there is a risk of possibly exacerbating mental health symptoms when CISD and related approaches are applied. Methods of Psychological First Aid (PFA) have been endorsed by groups of experts as an alternative to stress debriefing for immediate response in the first hours and days post-incident.

PFA is not an adequate post-incident response. Rather it should be part of a more comprehensive set of activities that would also include survivor education, ongoing monitoring and follow-up, and referral for more intensive services as needed. Such comprehensive approaches have sometimes been called Critical Incident Stress Management.

Keep in mind none of the information provided in this section should take the place of specialized training in the field.

5.7.2.1. Purpose of Behavioral Health Response

Behavioral health responses to traumatic events should form part of an integrated system of services and procedures with a purpose to achieve several goals:

- Prevention of traumatic stress;
- Mitigation of traumatic stress;
- Intervention to assist in recovery from traumatic stress;
- Acceleration of recovery whenever possible;
- Restoration to function; and
- Maintenance of worker health and welfare.

5.7.2.2. The Response Team

A Response team, generally comprised of mental health professionals and trained peer support personnel, provides a variety of services including:

- Psychological First Aid;
- Defusings;
- Demobilizations after a disaster;
- Informal discussions;
- Significant other support services;
- Work support groups;
- Individual consults (one-on-one); and
- Follow-up services.

For the purposes of this discussion, the focus will be on Psychological First Aid (PFA).

5.7.3. The Psychological First Aid Model

The impact of a critical incident on an individual's life appears to be mitigated, to some degree, by the availability of intervention resources used at various stages following the incident. The PFA model assists the victims of critical incidents with their recovery process.

The PFA model involves a set of core actions, described below:

1. Contact and Engagement

Goal: Respond to contacts initiated by affected persons or initiate contacts in a non-intrusive, compassionate, and helpful manner.

2. Safety and Comfort

Goal: Enhance immediate and ongoing safety and provide physical and emotional comfort.

3. Stabilization (if needed)

Goal: Calm and orient emotionally-overwhelmed/distraught survivors.

4. Information Gathering: Current Needs and Concerns

Goal: Identify immediate needs and concerns, gather additional information, and tailor PFA interventions.

5. Practical Assistance

Goal: To offer practical help to the survivor in addressing immediate needs and concerns.

6. Connection with Social Supports

Goal: To help establish opportunities for brief or ongoing contacts with primary support persons or other sources of support, including family members, friends, and community helping resources.

7. Information on Coping

Goal: To provide information (about stress reactions and coping) to reduce distress and promote adaptive functioning.

8. Linkage with Collaborative Services

Goal: To link survivors with needed services, and inform them about available services that may be needed in the future.

These core goals of PFA constitute the basic objectives of providing early assistance (e.g., within days or weeks following an event). They will need to be addressed in a flexible way, using strategies that meet the specific needs of affected groups. The amount of time spent on each goal will vary from person to person and with different circumstances according to need.

5.7.4. Is a Behavioral Health Response Warranted?

One determination to make is whether a formal behavioral health response consultation with mental health experts is warranted. Though not all-inclusive, some examples of important questions to explore when assessing the need for such a response are these:

- What is the nature of the incident?
- Is the incident of sufficient magnitude as to cause significant emotional distress among those involved?
- How many individuals are affected by the incident?
- What signs and symptoms of distress are being displayed by the witnesses to the incident?
- Are the signs and symptoms growing worse as time passes?
- Are any of the following key indicators of a need for a response present: behavior change, regression, continued symptoms, intensifying symptoms, new symptoms arising, or group symptoms?

As these and other questions are explored, some instances may not warrant a formal debriefing. There may be a decision to briefly meet with the group(s) affected by the incidents to further assess the need for a formal debriefing. Under these circumstances, a critical incident stress defusing may be appropriate.

5.7.5. Conclusion

Although it is well established that incidents of workplace violence and other traumatic events can sometimes lead to development of post-traumatic stress disorder and other problems in some survivors, the effectiveness of PFA and other early interventions after these events is less clear. CISD has been shown not to prevent mental health problems, but PFA, although based on expert consensus, has not yet been tested in research. PFA and other educational and supportive methods should be employed following potentially traumatic events, and delivered by trained mental health professionals and other trained behavioral response team personnel.

6.0. ACKNOWLEDGMENTS

Contributors to the ISC *Violence in the Federal Workplace: A Guide for Prevention and Response* (ISC, 2012)

6.1. Organizations Participating in the ISC Working Groups

- Chief Human Capital Officers Council
- Department of Commerce/Office of Security
- Department of Defense/Defense Information Systems Agency
- Department of Health and Human Services
- Department of Homeland Security/Federal Protective Service
- Department of Labor/Occupational Safety and Health Administration
- Department of Veterans Affairs
- National Institute for Occupational Safety and Health
- Office of Personnel Management
- Uniform Services University of the Health Sciences
- United States Postal Inspection Service
- United States Postal Service

ISC Chair
Caitlin Durkovich
Assistant Secretary for Infrastructure Protection
U.S. Department of Homeland Security

ISC Executive Director
Austin Smith
Office of Infrastructure Protection
U.S. Department of Homeland Security

ISC Working Group Members and Contributors (2010 – 2012)

Bernard Holt
DHS Interagency Security Committee

Michelle B. Baker-Dubbs
Federal Deposit Insurance Corporation

Jeffrey Cavanaugh
DHS Interagency Security Committee

David Drummond, Ph.D.
Veterans Health Administration

Lynn Van Male, Ph.D.
Veterans Health Administration

Michael Hodgson, MD
Veterans Health Administration

Marie L'Etoile
Office of Personnel Management

Ingrid Burford
Office of Personnel Management

James Gallagher
Department of Interior

Alexis Adams-Shorter, Ph.D.
Office of Personnel Management

Teresa Williams
Office of Personnel Management

Jeffrey Jenkins
Department of Homeland Security

Javier Perez
Office of Personnel Management

Josef I. Ruzek, Ph.D.
Veterans Health Administration

ISC Working Group Members (2008-2009)

Daniel Hartley
HHS NIOSH

Ronald Martin
Department of Health and Human Services

Harlan Amandus
HHS/NIOSH

Timothy Bane
DHS Federal Protective Service

Gregory Barber, Sr.
Department of Labor/OSHA

Patricia Billeter
Department of Commerce

Mike Bryan
DHS Interagency Security Committee

Brian Farrow
DHS Federal Protective Service

Paula Grubb
HHS NIOSH

Sydney Smith-Heimbrock
Office of Personnel Management

Gwainevere Hess
DHS Interagency Security Committee

Jerome Huggins
United States Postal Inspection Service

Marie L'Etoile
Office of Personnel Management

Jeanne Majidi
DHS Interagency Security Committee

Donna Peterson
United States Postal Service

Lucy Polk
Office of Personnel Management

Shanika Ratliff
Department of Commerce

Susan Reider
Department of Health and Human Services

Timothy Sullivan
Department of Defense

Mary Tyler
Uniform Services University of the Health Sciences

List of Abbreviations/Acronyms/Initializations

ADR	Alternative Dispute Resolution
ATAP	Association of Threat Assessment Professionals
CFR	Code of Federal Regulations
CISD	Critical Incident Stress Debriefing
DHS	Department of Homeland Security
EAP	Employee Assistance Program
EEOC	Equal Employment Opportunity Commission
EO	Executive Order
FSC	Facility Security Committee
FSL	Facility Security Level
F. 2d	Federal Reporter, Second Edition
FBI	Federal Bureau of Investigation
FPS	Federal Protective Service
GSA	General Services Administration
HCR	Historical Clinical Risk Management
HHS	Department of Health and Human Services
HSPD	Homeland Security Presidential Directive
ISC	Interagency Security Committee
MSPB	Merit System Protection Board MSPR Merit System Protection Reporter
NIOSH	National Institute for Occupational Safety and Health
OEP	Occupant Emergency Plan
OGC	Office of General Counsel
OIG	Office of the Inspector General
OPM	Office of Personnel Management
OSHA	Occupational Safety and Health Administration
PFA	Psychological First Aid
PMDB	Prevention and Management of Disruptive Behavior
PSOP	Physical Security Outreach Program
USC	United States Code
VHA	Veterans Health Administration
WAVR	Workplace Assessment of Violence Risk

APPENDIX A: THREAT ASSESSMENT, COUNTERMEASURES, AWARENESS, RESOURCES, AND CASE STUDIES

Please see the attached Appendix A stand-alone document.

End Notes

[1] For the 2011 crime statistics, please see the FBI web site at www.fbi.gov/news/pressrel/press-releases/fbi-releases-2011- crime-statistics, accessed March 29, 2013.

[2] For the BLS statistics, please see the BLS web site at www.bls.gov/iif/oshwc/cfoi/osar 0016.htm, accessed March 29, 2013.

[3] (BLS, 2005)

[4] (California/Occupational Safety and Health Administration, 1995; University of Iowa, 2001)

[5] (Department of Labor [DOL], 2002)

[6] (Meloy JR. Empirical basis and forensic application of affective and predatory violence. Aust N Z J Psychiatry. 2006 JunJul;40(6-7):539-47)

[7] 29 USC §651 et. seq.

[8] http://www.justice.gov/; search document title as location periodically changes.

[9] Please see the main FBI web site at www.fbi.gov/about-us/cirg/investigations-and-operations-support, and also see www.fbi.gov/stats-services/publications/workplace-violence, accessed March 29, 2013.

[10] Webster, C., and others, *HCR-20: Assessing Risk for Violence, Version 2*. Burnaby, British Columbia, Canada: Mental Health, Law, and Policy Institute, Simon Fraser University, 1997. http://www.minddisorders.com/Flu-Inv/Historical-Clinical-Risk-Management-20. html

[11] WAVR (Workplace Assessment of Violence Risk)-21: A New Instrument for Assessing Workplace Violence Risk is a 21-item coded instrument for the structured assessment of workplace targeted violence risk. http://www.wavr21.com/brief.html

[12] For more information, please see the VA web site at www.publichealth.va.gov /employeehealth/threatmanagement/index.aspand www.prevention.va.gov/VHA_ Prevention_Policies_and_Guidelines.asp, accessed March 29, 2013.

[13] Please see the FEMA web site at www.training.fema.gov/EMIWeb/IS/courseOverview.aspx? code=IS-106.13, accessed March 29, 2013

[14] Derived from *Kalkines v United States*, 473 F. 2d 1391 (Ct. Cl. 1973).

[15] See *National Labor Relations Board v. Weingarten*, Inc., 420 US 251 (1075)

[16] See *Hillen v. Army*, 35 MSPR 453 (1987).

[17] ATAP 2006

[18] Series: NIJ Research in Action, Published: September 1995, NCJ 155000. Disclaimer: Points of view in this document are those of the authors and do not necessarily reflect the official position of the U. S. Department of Justice.

[19] Dietz, P. E. and D. A. Martell, Mentally Disordered Offenders in Pursuit of Celebrities and Politicians, National Institute of Justice, Washington, D. C., 1989, 83-NI-AX-0005; Dietz, P. E., D. B. Matthews, D. A. Martell, T. M. Stewart, D. R. Hrouda and J. Warren,

Threatening and Otherwise Inappropriate Letters to Members of the United States Congress, Journal of Forensic Sciences, 36 (September 5, 1991): 1445-1468; Dietz, P. E., D. B. Matthews, C. Van Duyne, D. A. Martell, C. D. H. Parry, T. M. Stewart, J. Warren and J. D. Crowder, Threatening and Otherwise Inappropriate Letters to Hollywood Celebrities, Journal of Forensic Sciences, 36 (January 1, 1991): 185-209; and Fein, R. A. and B. Vossekuil, The Secret Service Exceptional Case Study Project: An Examination of Violence Against Public Officials and Public Figures, National Institute of Justice, study in progress, 92-CX-0013.

[20] For example, both Thomas McIlvane, in the Royal Oak, Michigan post office attack, and Alan Winterbourne, in the Oxnard, California unemployment office attack, killed themselves.

[21] http://www.secretservice.gov/ntac/PI_Guide.pdf

[22] 5 USC §7513(a), 01/03/2012 (112-90); 5 USC §7701(c)(1)(b) 01/03/2012 (112-90) and 5 CFR §752 (01/01/2005)

[23] 5 CFR §7513(b) 01/03/2012 (112-90)

[24] Available at http://www.eeoc.gov

[25] 5 CFR §339.301 – 302 (01/01/2011)

[26] 5 CFR §831.501(d) (02/04/2013) http://www.ecfr.gov/cgi-bin/text-idx?c=ecfr&SID=f8a9bc18af98e4a9411a1f39862256c1&rgn=div5&view=text&node=5:2.0.1.1.18&idn o=55

[27] 5 CFR §831.1201-1206 (02/04/2013) (covering CSRS employees). For FERS employees, see 5 CFR §844.202 (01/01/2012).

In: Acts of Violence in the Federal Workplace
Editor: Felix Tash
ISBN: 978-1-62808-172-5

Chapter 2

VIOLENCE IN THE FEDERAL WORKPLACE: A GUIDE FOR PREVENTION AND RESPONSE, APPENDIX A: THREAT ASSESSMENTS, COUNTERMEASURES, AWARENESS, AND CASE STUDIES*

Interagency Security Committee

1.0. RISK MANAGEMENT PROCESS

The nature of criminal and terrorist threats to Federal facilities and employees has changed substantially over time, and it is management's job to ensure the effectiveness of protective measures changes as well. Employees want to know what the agency is doing to protect them and their facilities and what measures to take to protect themselves. Since it is impossible to know with any certainty whether a threat is going to be carried out, the agency should always approach facility and employee security in a serious manner and prepare as though a potential or known threat will evolve into a hostile act.

Physical security of nonmilitary Federal employees, contractors, visitors and facilities, has improved since the April 1995 attack on the Alfred P. Murrah Federal Building in Oklahoma City with the creation of the

* This is an edited, reformatted and augmented version of Interagency Security Committee, dated April 2013.

Interagency Security Committee (ISC). President Clinton issued Executive Order 12977[1] establishing the ISC that is today a component within the Department of Homeland Security. The ISC is a permanent body with representatives from over 50 Federal agencies and departments working together to address continuing government-wide security needs for Federal facilities. It establishes minimum security standards and oversees implementation of countermeasures to address current and future risks; thus, helping ensure the safety and security of nonmilitary Federal facilities and the individuals within them from all-hazards.

The ISC designed a process to identify an achievable level of protection commensurate with the level of risk posed to a nonmilitary Federal facility in the United States. The process involves:

- Determining the appropriate Facility Security Level (FSL);
- Identifying the baseline Level of Protection (LOP) and countermeasures;
- Identifying and assessing risks;
- Determining the LOP required to address risks or the highest achievable LOP;
- Implementing countermeasures; and
- Measuring performance.

A facility with a high FSL will naturally require a greater level of protection, while a facility with a lower FSL faces a lower risk and does not require the same LOP as a facility with a higher FSL. Furthermore, the ISC developed the *Design-Basis Threat Report*[2] for official use only (FOUO), a standalone threat document to be included in the ISC risk management process. The DBT establishes a profile of the types, composition, and capabilities of adversaries. The DBT establishes the characteristics of the threat environment to be used in conjunction with ISC security standards. The design-basis threat (DBT) supports the calculation of the threat, vulnerability, and consequence to a facility when calculating risk to a Federal facility and determining the appropriate LOP. In addition, the DBT determines specific adversary characteristics that performance standards and countermeasures are designed to overcome.

The ISC produced standards documents to aid security managers and facility security committees through the risk management process. In addition to reports and guidelines related to risk and threat assessment and the facility risk management process, the ISC also publishes best practices guidelines for things such as safe mail screening, and proper training and equipping of security personnel. The ISC designated the majority of these documents as FOUO to prevent distribution to malicious actors. For this reason, authorized users may access the standards as they are published through the Homeland Security Information Network or by contacting the ISC at ISCAccess@dhs.gov.

2.0. WORKPLACE VIOLENCE RISK/THREAT ASSESSMENT

A workplace "risk assessment" examines the physical facilities, the surrounding environment, and every function or job performed onsite to identify and quantify both real and perceived security risks. The assessment process involves:

- Reviewing injury data and policies;
- Reviewing incident reports and records (including safety and security);
- Requests for staff input; and
- Performing a thorough inspection of the physical property.

The final product of a workplace risk assessment identifies both the risks and the methods used to reduce or eliminate the risks. In addition, the assessment assists in establishing and/or maintaining a performance measurement cycle to enhance decision-making on the allocation of resources in the attempt to prevent attacks upon personnel and/or facilities.

A risk assessment for workplace violence evaluates who may be exposed, when and how often the exposure is likely to occur, and under what conditions. The purpose of the assessment is to enable the employer to implement any measures necessary to protect the agency's workforce. Rating the assessed risks as high or low will help determine priorities for implementing risk management strategies. For example, the risk of violence may be considered high if it happens frequently (e.g., customer service disputes) or if the consequences are potentially severe (e.g., armed robbery).

Some common components of a workplace violence risk assessment include:

2.1. Staff Input

- Interview staff in the agency to determine if and under what circumstances violence occurred in the past.
- Ask employees about their safety concerns and how they dealt with incidents or threats of violence.
- Gather information through confidential surveys; this may be the most effective method to compile complete and unbiased information.
- Survey employees to get their ideas on the occurrence and potential for violent incidents; help identify jobs, locations, or work situations where the risk of violence appears highest; and to identify or confirm the need for improved security measures.
- Repeat surveys at regular intervals or as necessary.

NOTE: Employee information and feedback is the most important component of the risk assessment process.

2.2. Current Practice Review

- Thoroughly review the agency's current safety programs and procedures such as:
  - Occupant emergency plans;
  - Harassment policies;
  - Hiring and termination practices; and
  - Task-specific safety procedures.
- Check to be certain the following items are adequate:
  - Inputs and process measures of budgetary resources;
  - Human capital;
  - Materials and services; and
  - Facilities and equipment.
- Check to be certain the risk management functions and activities undertaken are correctly geared toward achieving the objective.

2.3. Data Analysis

Use security reports and information from the staff interviews/surveys to determine who is exposed to potential violence, the type of interpersonal interactions or tasks that may lead to violent incidents, the circumstances of such incidents, and the usual or likely outcome. Ensure the outcomes or results represent the impact of the organization upon its customers or problems in such a way as to achieve the desired workplace conditions and prevent undesired conditions or incidents.

2.4. Strategy Development

Choose strategies that best manage the risks identified for the agency. Some strategies may include:

- Develop or revise general- and task-specific safety procedures; and
- Revise staff training and consider scheduling a special session to discuss issues found in the risk assessment.

The DBT provides specific details as to the characteristics of each event that might take place at a Federal facility. They are based on a worst-reasonable-case basis. A baseline threat rating is provided, and target attractiveness characteristics that may make a facility more or less attractive as a target are enumerated as appropriate. Each event provides sufficient information from which the threat, consequences, and vulnerability can be extrapolated while conducting a risk assessment. In addition, in estimating the threat level, specific information unique to the facility or the locale may be used. Local crime statistics, the tactics of adversary groups known to be operating in a particular area, and other actionable intelligence that suggests a different threat level may modify the threat from the baseline. Event documents may be updated or replaced, and undesirable events may be added in order to maintain the applicability of the DBT.

3.0. Threat Assessment Team

Many Federal agencies established threat assessment teams, a multi-disciplinary group of individuals trained to assist in assessing the potential for workplace violence incidents and the best methods for preventing their escalation. These teams often go through specialized training that usually includes table top exercises designed to simulate potential workplace violence or facility preparedness scenarios. The threat assessment team should also schedule initial and recurring risk assessments and the accompanying FSL determination. Tracking and measuring the completed assessments against planned activities for the time frame demonstrates management's continuous commitment to maintaining a systemic physical security program. The combination of attention to personal and physical asset security shows the threat assessment team is an integral part of an advanced workplace violence prevention program.

4.0. COUNTERMEASURES

Many countermeasures form the front-line defense for preventing violence from occurring in the workplace. Examples include:

- Building access controls;
- Alarm systems;
- Video surveillance systems;
- Magnetometers and x-ray machines;
- Security/police presence; and
- Unique badges/photo identification.

In some cases, the on-site Federal law enforcement or security entity charged with protecting a facility may provide assistance with restraining orders/documents involving domestic violence situations, helping to keep employees and visitors safe from known threats. However, no single countermeasure can effectively negate all risks. The degree of measures' effectiveness can be enhanced with regular testing to determine how well they work. Testing encompasses such elements as determining if equipment is calibrated properly, security guards are knowledgeable in post-order procedures, and if intrusion detection systems are activating properly. Testing could also include planned exercises to try and breach security to ensure existing countermeasures are capable of securing the facility against an established set of testing protocols.

The most important countermeasure is intelligence/information and remains the foundation for effective risk assessment and facility protection issues. All employees are responsible for maintaining an awareness of their surroundings to include co-workers and patrons. Any warning signs an employee notices in co-workers or patrons should be appropriately reported and investigated.

5.0. AWARENESS

5.1. Threat Awareness

Many Federal agencies have awareness programs in place to educate the Federal workforce about preventing workplace violence. Employees should not only recognize the four classic types of workplace violence described previously (i.e.., criminal intent, customer/client, employee-on-employee, and personal relationship), but should also be aware of other possible precursor behaviors to violent acts in the workplace. Workplace aggression may involve more subtle acts of incivility or emotional abuse, or may take the more overt form of intimidation or hostility. These types of negative behaviors may pose a risk to others, especially if they occur frequently over a given period of time. This persistent, systematic mistreatment of an individual or individuals in the workplace is referred to as workplace bullying. Employees also need to be aware of potential issues that could result in workplace violence such as problems among employees or behaviors suggesting a possible violence issue. For example, victims of domestic violence may have frequent, unexplained absences or wear seasonally inappropriate clothing to cover injuries. Perpetrators of domestic violence may commit cyber-stalking by obsessively telephoning, texting, or e-mailing their target throughout the work day.

In addition to examining threat assessment at the individual level, an effective workplace violence prevention and response plan must address threats at the agency and/or facility level and prepare in accordance with the facility's established FSL. For detailed information regarding the FSL determination process, including the scoring system and criteria used in assessing scores, see *Facility Security Level Determinations for Federal Facilities.*[3]

Threat to tenant agencies is considered from a perspective of target attractiveness. The facility should be viewed in terms of whether the nature of public contact required in or resulting from the conduct of business is adversarial, and any history of adversarial acts committed at the facility, against facility tenants, or against the tenant agencies elsewhere. The highest score applicable to any tenant in a multi-tenant facility will be considered when determining the FSL, even though it may be possible to limit the implementation of countermeasures for that threat to a specific tenant's space or part of the facility.

As with the impact of commercial tenants on the facility's symbolism score, the potential threat to non-Federal tenants in a mixed-tenant or mixed-multi-tenant facility could result in a collateral risk to Federal tenants. Thus, in considering the criteria, the threat to all tenants in a facility— including non-Federal tenants—should be considered and the highest score used for the rating.

It is not possible for this document to take into account all the conditions that may affect the FSL determination for all the different Federal departments and agencies. Certain factors, such as a short duration of occupancy, may reduce the "value" of a facility in terms of investment or mission; therefore, such a factor could justify a reduction of the FSL. Such factors are in essence indicative of a reduced value of the facility itself and a corresponding reduction in the consequences of its loss.

Other factors may suggest an increase in the FSL, such as the potential for cascading effects or downstream impacts on interdependent infrastructure, or costs associated with the reconstitution of the facility. Accordingly, the FSL may be raised or lowered one level at the discretion of the deciding authority based on intangible factors. However, the intangible factor should not be used to raise or lower the FSL in response to a particular threat act. The FSL characterizes the entire facility; concerns about specific threats should be addressed with specific countermeasures, even if they are over and above those required as the baseline for a particular security level.

Short-term incidents could also temporarily affect the factors evaluated here. Unless these incidents happen on a recurring basis, they should not affect the FSL determination. Instead, contingency plans should be developed to implement temporary measures until the incident has passed.

5.2. Active Shooter Preparedness

[Note: The following section was drawn largely from the DHS website regarding Active Shooters (http://www.dhs.gov/active-shooter-preparedness).]

The Department of Homeland Security (DHS) aims to enhance preparedness through a "whole community" approach by providing training, products, and resources to a broad range of stakeholders on issues such as active shooter awareness, incident response, and workplace violence. In many cases, there is no pattern or method to the selection of victims by an active shooter, and these situations are by their very nature are unpredictable and evolve quickly. DHS offers free courses, materials, and workshops to better prepare the public to deal with an active shooter situation and to raise awareness of behaviors that represent pre-incident indicators and characteristics of active shooters.

Topics and resources covered include:

- Active Shooter: What Can You Do Course
- Active Shooter Webinar
- Active Shooter Workshop Series
- Active Shooter: How to Respond Resource Materials
- Options for Consideration Active Shooter Training Video
- U.S. Secret Service (USSS) Active Shooter Related Research
- Active Shooter Resources for Law Enforcement and Trainers: Request for Access to Joint Countering Violent Extremism (CVE) Portal

5.2.1. Active Shooter: What You Can Do Course

DHS developed an Independent Study Course titled *Active Shooter: What You Can Do*. This course was developed to provide the public with guidance on how to prepare for and respond to active shooter crisis situations.

Upon completion of *Active Shooter: What You Can Do*, employees and managers will be able to:

- Describe the actions to take when confronted with an active shooter and to assist responding law enforcement officials;
- Recognize potential workplace violence indicators;
- Describe actions to take to prevent and prepare for potential active shooter incidents; and
- Describe how to manage the consequences of an active shooter incident.

The online training is available through the Federal Emergency Management Agency Emergency Management Institute (http://training.fema.gov/EMIWeb/IS/IS907.asp) and additional training for law enforcement is available at Federal Emergency Management Agency Law Enforcement Active Shooter Emergency Response (http://www.ncbrt.lsu.edu/catalog/performance/laser.aspx).

5.2.2. Active Shooter Webinar

A 90-minute Webinar (http://connect.hsin.gov/asaware2011) can help the private and public sector understand the importance of developing an emergency response plan and the need to train employees on how to respond if confronted with an active shooter. The presentation describes the three types of active shooters: workplace/school, criminal, and ideological--and how their planning cycles and behaviors differ.

5.2.3. Active Shooter Workshop Series

Active Shooter workshops already took place in a number of U.S. cities and will continue to be held in a number of locations in the future. These scenario-based workshops feature facilitated discussions to engage private sector professionals and law enforcement representatives from Federal, state, and local agencies to learn how to prepare for, and respond to, an active shooter situation. Through the course of the exercise, participants evaluate current response concepts, plans, and capabilities for coordinated responses to active shooter incidents.

If you are interested in future workshops, please contact ASworkshop@hq.dhs.gov.

5.2.4. Active Shooter: How to Respond Resource Materials

DHS developed a series of materials to assist businesses, government offices, and schools in preparing for and responding to an active shooter. These products include a desk reference guide, a reference poster, and a pocket-size reference card.

Issues covered in the active shooter materials include the following:

- Profile of an active shooter;
- Responding to an active shooter or other workplace violence situation;
- Training for an active shooter situation and creating an emergency action plan; and
- Tips for recognizing signs of potential workplace violence.

Available Materials:

- Active Shooter Booklet

(http://www.dhs.gov/xlibrary/assets/active shooter booklet.pdf)

- Active Shooter Poster

(http://www.dhs.gov/xlibrary/assets/active shooter poster.pdf)

- Active Shooter Poster (Spanish)
(http://www.dhs.gov/xlibrary/assets/active-shooter-poster-spanish.pdf)
- Active Shooter Pocket Card
(http://www.dhs.gov/xlibrary/assets/active shooter pocket card.pdf)
- Active Shooter Pocket Card (Spanish)
(http://www.dhs.gov/xlibrary/assets/active-shooter-pocket-spanish.pdf)

5.2.5. Options for Consideration Active Shooter Training Video

The Options for Consideration (http://www.dhs.gov/video/options-consideration-active-shootertraining-video) video demonstrates possible actions to take if confronted with an active shooter scenario. The instructive video reviews the choices of evacuating, hiding, or, as an option of last resort, challenging the shooter. The video also shows how to assist authorities once law enforcement enters the scene.

You may also access the video on YouTube.

5.2.6. U.S. Secret Service Active Shooter Related Research

The U.S. Secret Service (USSS) makes available a number of resources regarding active shooters:

- Campus Attacks: Targeted Violence Affecting Institutions of Higher Education(http://www.secretservice.gov/ntac/CampusAttacks041610.pdf)
- Prior Knowledge of Potential School-Based Violence: Information Students Learn May Prevent a Targeted Attack (http://www.secretservice.gov/ntac/bystander study.pdf)
- Assassination in the United States: An Operational Study of Recent Assassins, Attackers, and Near Lethal Approaches (http://www.secretservice.gov/ntac/ntac jfs.pdf)
- Protective Intelligence & Threat Assessment Investigations: A Guide for State and Local Law Enforcement Officials (http://www.secretservice.gov/ntac/PI Guide.pdf)
- Threat Assessment: An Approach to Prevent Targeted Violence (http://www.secretservice.gov/ntac/ntac threat.pdf)
- Threat Assessment: Defining an Approach for Evaluating Risk of Targeted Violence (http://www.secretservice.gov/ntac/ntac bsl99.pdf)

For more information on USSS programs, please visit http://www .secretservice.gov/ntac.shtml.

5.2.7. Active Shooter Resources for Law Enforcement and Trainers: Request for Access to Joint Countering Violent Extremism Portal

DHS, in partnership with the Federal Bureau of Investigation (FBI) and the International Association of Chiefs of Police, has launched a CVE Training Resource web portal on the Homeland Security Information Network (HSIN). The purpose is to provide federal, state, local, tribal, territorial, and correctional law enforcement with the most current CVE training materials, case studies, analytic products, and other resources. The materials on the portal are restricted for law enforcement training use only and will contain unclassified/FOUO/law enforcement sensitive information.

To request access to the Joint CVE Portal, send an email to CVEPortal@HQ.DHS.gov. In the subject line, write "Request for Access to Joint CVE Portal." In the body of the email, please provide your full name, email address, business phone, and organization/agency.

6.0. Resources

6.1. Federal Government Offices

Office of Personnel Management (OPM)
Agencies Employee Relations and Health Services Center
1900 E Street, NW
Washington, DC 20415
(202) 606-1858

OPM's Employee Relations and Health Services Center provides advice and assistance to Federal agencies on issues relating to employee relations and Employee Assistance Program policy, including workplace violence, traumatic incidents, reasonable accommodation, and discipline. OPM publications include:

- A Manager's Handbook: Handling Traumatic Events is available through the OPM rider system.
- Significant Cases, a bi-monthly summary of important decisions of the courts, the U. S. Merit Systems Protection Board, and the Federal Labor Relations Authority is available through the OPM rider system.
- Alternative Dispute Resolution: A Resource Guide is available by calling the phone number listed above.

Department of Health and Human Services (HHS) Centers for Disease Control and Prevention

National Institute for Occupational Safety and Health (NIOSH)
Robert A. Taft Laboratories
4676 Columbia Parkway
Cincinnati, OH 45226-1998
(800) 356-4674

NIOSH issued a publication on workplace violence, *Violence in the Workplace: Risk Factors and Prevention Strategies*, (NIOSH Current Intelligence Bulletin No. 57 Publication Number 96- 100), June 1996. To obtain a copy, call the toll free number or access through the Internet at http://www.cdc.gov/niosh/violrisk.html.

Callers may also use the toll free number to find a directory of topics of publications and databases that may be ordered. Recorded summaries providing overviews and relevant statistics about selected topics are also available. Use the automated fax information service to receive documents within 15 minutes. Technical information specialists may also be reached on this number from 9:00 AM to 4:00 PM Eastern time, Monday through Friday. Callers may also learn about NIOSH training resources or request a NIOSH workplace health hazard evaluation. Access through the Internet at www.cdc.gov/niosh/homepage.html.

Department of Justice

National Institute of Justice
National Criminal Justice Reference Service
Bureau of Justice Assistance Clearinghouse (BJAC)
P. O. Box 6000
Rockville, MD 20849-6000
(800) 851-3420

Calling the toll free number offers several information options including a fax-on-demand service for documents, being able to speak with a specialist, or learning about how to access an electronic newsletter through their web and email address. The caller can also learn about their Research and Information Center located in Rockville, Maryland. BJAC also has a catalog of National Institute of Justice documents. Many of the documents included in the catalog pertain to workplace violence, for example: *Violence and Theft in the Workplace*; *The Cycle of Violence; Psychoactive Substances and Violence*;

and *Crime Prevention through Environmental Design in Parking Facilities* can be accessed through the Internet at https://www.ncjrs.gov/.

Department of Labor
Occupational Safety and Health Administration (OSHA)
200 Constitution Avenue, NW, Room N3107
Washington, DC 20210
General information: (202) 219-8031
Publications: (202) 219-4667

OSHA's published *Guidelines for Preventing Workplace Violence for Health Care and Social Service Workers*, U. S. Department of Labor, Occupational Safety and Health Administration, (OSHA 3148), 1996. Copies may be obtained from the Government Printing Office by calling (202) 512-1800 or access through the Internet at http://www.osha.gov /Publications /OSHA3148/osha3148.html.

Contact OSHA's Office of Federal Agency Programs (FAP) at (202) 219-9329 to obtain information on OSHA record-keeping and reporting requirements for Federal agencies (OSHA Instruction FAP 1.3).

Department of Labor
Women's Bureau
200 Constitution Avenue, NW - Room S-3002
Washington, DC 20210
(202) 693-6710

The Women's Bureau issued *Domestic Violence: A Workplace Issue*, October 1996, Document Number 96-3.

6.2. Federal Government Online Resources

Bureau of Labor Statistics, *Census of Fatal Occupational Injuries* is available Online: http://www.bls.gov/iif/#tables.

Bureau of Justice Statistics, *National Crime Victimization Survey: Violence in the Workplace 1993-99*, December 2001." Available Online: http://bjs.ojp.usdoj.gov/content/pub/pdf/vw99.pdf.

Department of Agriculture (USDA), *the USDA Handbook on Workplace Violence Prevention and Response*, December 1998.

Department of Health and Human Services (HHS), Centers for Disease Control and Prevention, *Emergency Preparedness and Response*. Available Online: http://www.bt.cdc.gov/planning/shelteringfacts.asp .

Department of Labor, *Recommendations for Workplace Violence Prevention Programs in Late Night Retail Establishments.* (OSHA 3153 - 2009): Available online: http://www.osha.gov/Publications/osha3153.pdf.

Executive Order 10450, *Security Requirements for Government Employment*. April 27, 1953. Available Online: http://www.archives.gov /federal-register/codification/executiveorder/10450.html.

Executive Order 12196, *Occupational Safety and Health Programs for Federal employees*. February 26, 1980. Available Online: http://www. archives.gov/federalregister/codification/executive-order/12196.html.

Executive Order 12977, *Interagency Security Committee*. October 19, 1995. Available Online: http://frwebgate.access.gpo.gov/cgi-bin/getdoc.cgi? dbname=1995 register&docid=fr24oc95- 145.pdf.

Federal Bureau of Investigations (FBI), *Workplace Violence - Issues in Response*, Critical Incident Response Group, National Center for the Analysis of Violent Crime, FBI Academy, Quantico, VA. March 2004. Available Online: http://www.fbi.gov/statsservices/publications/workplace-violence.

General Services Administration. Federal Protective Service, *Occupant Emergency Plan Guide*. November 2007. Available Online: http://www.gsa.gov/graphics/pbs/OEP Guide.pdf.

Homeland Security Presidential Directive – 12, *Policy for a Common Identification Standard for Federal Employees and Contractors*. August 27, 2004. Available Online: http://www.dhs.gov/xabout/laws/gc 1217616624 097.shtm.

Merit Systems Protection Board, *the Probationary Period: A Critical Assessment Opportunity*. August 2005. Available Online: http://www.mspb. gov/netsearch/viewdocs.aspx?docnumber=224555&version=224774&applicat i on=ACROBAT.

NIOSH, Publication No. 2006-144: *Workplace Violence Prevention Strategies and Research Needs*. Available Online: http://www.cdc.gov/niosh /docs/2006-144/.

OPM, *Dealing with Workplace Violence a Guide for Agency Planners*. February 1998.

Available Online: http://www.opm.gov/Employment and Benefits/Work Life/OfficialDocuments/handbooksguides /WorkplaceViolence/index.asp.

Occupational Safety and Health Act of 1970 - Public Law 91-596. December 29, 1970. Available Online: http://www.osha.gov/pls/oshaweb /owadisp.showdocument?p table=OSHACT&p id=2743.

6.3. Non-Federal Government Organizations

The following list is not exhaustive of the organizations available, nor does the list constitute an endorsement by OPM or the Interagency Security Committee.

American Psychiatric Association (APA) 1000 Wilson Boulevard, suite 1825 Arlington, VA 22209

The APA publishes a free fact sheet, *Violence and Mental Illness*, Document Number 6109. To obtain a copy, call the APA's fast fax automatic document retrieval service at (888) 267-5400 or access through the Internet at www.psych.org/ (listed under Resources for the General Public, Fact Sheet Series).

American Psychological Association 750 First Street, NE

Washington, DC 20002

(202) 336-5500

Information on violence is available on the association's website at www.apa.org/.

International Association of Chiefs of Police (IACP) 515 North Washington Street Alexandria, VA 22314-2357

The IACP has published a booklet, *Combating Workplace Violence: Guidelines for Employers and Law Enforcement*. To obtain a copy, write to the IACP at the address above or access the Internet at http://www.theiacp.org /Portals/0/pdfs/Publications/combatingworkplaceviolence.pdf.

International Critical Incident Stress Foundation 3290 Pine Orchard Lane, Suite 106

Ellicott City, MD 21042

(410) 750-9600

The International Critical Incident Stress Foundation provides information and training on critical incident stress management.

National Crime Prevention Council (NCPC) 2001 Jefferson Davis Highway, Suite 901 Arlington, VA 22202

(202) 466-6272

NCPC provides information on the prevention of crime and violence.

National Domestic Violence Hotline (800) 799-SAFE

(800) 787-3224 (TTY)

This nationwide hotline offers crisis intervention, problem-solving skills, information, and referral to service agency providers.

National Organization for Victim Assistance Organizations 510 King Street, Suite 424

Alexandria, VA 22314

(800) TRY-NOVA

The organization refers callers to local victim assistance organizations.

National Center for Victims of Crime (202) 467-8700

2000 M Street, NW, Suite 480

Washington, DC 20036

The National Center for Victims of Crime, accessible through the Internet at http://www.ncvc.org, provides information and referrals to local victim assistance organizations.

National Resource Center on Workplace Response to Domestic and Sexual Violence, http://www.workplacesrespond.org.

6.4. Non-Federal Government Online Resources

American Society of Industrial Security, *Workplace Violence Prevention and Response Guidelines*. March 2005.

California Division of Occupational Safety and Health, *Guidelines for Workplace Security*. 1995. Available Online: http://www.dir.ca.gov/dosh/dosh publications/worksecurity.html.

FedSmith.com, Steve Oppermann, *Workplace Bullying: Psychological Violence?* December 2008. Available Online: http://www.fedsmith.com/article /1780/workplace-bullyingpsychological-violence.html.

University of Iowa, *Workplace Violence: A Report to the Nation*. February 2001. Available Online: http://www.public-health.uiowa.edu/iprc /resources /workplace-violence-report.pdf.

Victims of Crime Act Victim Assistance and Victims Compensation. http://www.ojp.usdoj.gov/ovc/map.html.

6.5. Computer Systems

Partnership Against Violence Network (PAVNET), accessible through the Internet at www.pavnet.org, is a clearinghouse with over 500 entries on violence. Government and non-government organizations addressing the subject of violence are listed. Information in PAVNET includes:

- Funding grants;
- Research projects;
- Grass-roots efforts to address violence; and
- Curriculum development.

NOTE: Under Federal law, the OPM is prohibited from ranking, endorsing, or promoting agencies or organizations listed on its Website.

7.0. CASE STUDIES

The call comes in. Someone has been shot -- there is a fight going on -- someone has been threatened – someone has been stalked by an ex-boyfriend – someone is threatening suicide -- someone wants to put a stop to the "bullying" behavior that's been going on in his office.

These are just a few examples of the types of incidents reported.

How each agency responds to these reports will vary, not only among agencies but also within each agency since circumstances surrounding each situation are different. Even in highly-structured agencies with well-designed procedures in place, the response will necessarily depend on:

- The nature of the incident;
- The circumstances surrounding the incident;
- Personnel available to respond; and
- Personnel with the skills to deal with the particular situation.

A lesson learned from many years of experience is that the most effective way to manage these situations is to take a team approach, rather than having one office handle a situation alone. In three separate cases of workplace homicides, the situation escalated either because personnel specialists did not inform security about a problem employee, co-workers were not warned about the threatening behavior of an ex-employee, or an agency specialist felt they had to handle the situation on their own.

Agencies should have plans in place ahead of time so that emergency and non-emergency situations can be addressed as soon as possible. However, it is also necessary to build the maximum amount of flexibility possible into any plan.

7.1. Section 1: Basic Concepts

Since agencies and situations differ, specific steps or procedures to follow on a government-wide basis would be inappropriate and impractical. However, there are some basic concepts that all agencies should keep in mind when formulating their strategy to address workplace violence:

- Respond promptly to immediate dangers to personnel and the workplace;
- Investigate threats and other reported incidents;
- Take threats and threatening behavior seriously;
- Address issues even if they may appear to be frivolous allegations;
- Take disciplinary actions when warranted;
- Support victims and other affected workers after an incident; and
- Attempt to bring the work environment back to normal after an incident.

7.2. Section 2: How to Use the Case Studies

The case studies presented in this section are derived from real life situations experienced in Federal agencies. These are intended to provide assistance to agency planners as they develop workplace violence prevention and response programs, in addition to assessing their readiness to handle these types of situations. It should be noted the circumstances are modified in some of the case studies to make them better learning tools.

As you read the case studies, keep in mind there is no single correct way to address each situation. The case studies should not be taken as specific models of how to manage certain types of situations. Use these as a starting point for a discussion and exploration of how a team approach can be instituted and adapted to the specific needs and requirements of an agency.

Although these case studies are derived from real life situations, the characters in them are fictional and have been created for educational purposes. No reference to any individual, living or dead, is intended or should be inferred.

7.2.1. Questions for Discussion

The case studies are intended to raise questions such as:

- Do we agree with the approach the agency took in the case study?
- If not, why would that approach not work for us?
- Do we have adequate resources to handle such a situation?

7.2.2. Questions for Program Evaluation

Establish a system to evaluate the effectiveness of your response in actual situations that arise so you can change procedures if necessary. Ask the following questions after reviewing each of the case studies and after planning how your agency would respond to the same or a similar situation:

1) Does our workplace violence prevention and response program have a process for evaluating the effectiveness of the team's approach following an incident?
2) Would our written policy statement and procedures limit our ability to easily adopt a more effective course of action in the future, if an evaluation of our response showed that a change in procedures was necessary?
3) Do we have plans to test our response procedures and capabilities through practice exercises and preparedness drills and change procedures if necessary?

7.3. Case Study 1: Stalking

7.3.1. Incident

A supervisor called the employee relations office to request a meeting of the workplace violence team for assistance in handling a situation. He was counseling one of his employees about her frequent unscheduled absences, when she told him a chilling story of what she had been going through for the past year. She broke up with her boyfriend a year earlier, and he stalked her ever since. He called her several times a week, and she would hang up immediately. He would show up wherever she went on the weekends and would stare at her from a distance. He often parked his car down the block from her home and sat there. He made it known he had a gun.

7.3.2. Response

This agency's plan called for the initial involvement of security, Employee Assistance Program (EAP), and employee relations in cases involving stalking. The security officer, the EAP counselor, and employee relations specialist met first with the supervisor, and then with the employee and supervisor together. At the meeting with the employee, after learning as much of the background as possible, they gave her some initial suggestions:

- Contact her local police and file a report;
- Ask them to assess her security at home and make recommendations for improvements;
- Log all future contacts with the stalker and clearly record the date, time, and nature of the contact;
- Let voicemail screen incoming phone calls;
- Contact her phone company to report the situation;
- Give permission to let her co-workers know what was going on (she would not agree to do this); and
- Vary daily routine :
  - Go to different shop;
  - Take different routes;
  - Run errands at different times; and
  - Report to work on a variable schedule.
  - The team then created the following plan:

a) **Employee Relations Specialist:** acted as coordinator of the response effort. He made a written report of the situation and kept it updated. He kept the team members, the supervisor, and the employee apprised of what the others were doing to resolve the situation. He also looked into the feasibility of relocating the employee to another worksite.

b) **Security Officer:** reported the situation to the local police immediately. With the employee's consent, she also called the police where the employee lived to learn what steps they could take to help the employee. She offered to coordinate and exchange information with them. The security officer arranged for increased surveillance of the building and circulated photos of the stalker to all building guards with instructions to detain him if he showed up at the building. She brought a tape recorder to the employee's desk and showed her the best way to tape any future voice mail messages from the stalker. She also contacted the agency's phone company to arrange for its involvement in the case.

c) **EAP Counselor:** provided support and counseling for both the employee and the supervisor throughout the time this was going on. He suggested local organizations that could help the employee. He also tried to convince her to tell co-workers about the situation.
d) **The Union:** arranged to sponsor a session on stalking in order to raise the consciousness of agency employees about the problem in general.

After a week, when the employee finally agreed to tell co-workers what was going on, the EAP counselor and security officer jointly held a meeting with the whole work group to discuss any fears or concerns they had, and give advice on how they could help with the situation.

7.3.3. Resolution

In this case, the employee's co-workers were supportive and wanted to help. They volunteered to watch out for the stalker and to follow other security measures recommended by the security specialist. The stalker ended up in jail because he tried to break into the employee's home while armed with a gun. The security officer believed the local police were able to be more responsive in this situation because they had been working together with agency security on the case.

7.3.4. Questions for the Agency Planning Group

1) Do you agree with the agency's approach in this case?
2) What would you do in a similar situation if your agency does not have security guards?
3) What would you do if co-workers were too afraid of the stalker to work in the same office with the employee?
4) What would you do if/when the stalker gets out of jail on bail or probation?
5) Would your Office of the Inspector General (OIG) have gotten involved in this case (e.g., coordinated agency efforts with local law enforcement agencies)?

7.4. Case Study 2: Domestic Violence

7.4.1. Incident

The employee relations specialist received a phone call from an employee. The employee reported she just finished a long conversation with a co-worker who was a part-time employee and friend. Her co-worker revealed she was a victim of domestic violence. She learned the woman's husband began abusing her after their first child was born. Her husband was careful to injure her only in ways that did not leave visible signs, and she felt sure no one would ever believe her word against his. The family's assets, even her car, were all in his name, and her part-time salary would not have been enough to support her and the children. Further, he had threatened to kill her if she ever left him or revealed the abuse. After talking with the employee, the co-worker agreed to let the situation be reported to the workplace violence team.

7.4.2. Response

Employee Relations Specialist: agreed to meet with both employees immediately. At the employee relations specialist's suggestion, the abused woman asked to have her friend along and gave permission to explain the situation to the two employees' supervisor. After interviewing the abused woman in a caring, supportive way to get basic information, the employee relations specialist asked other team members, the security director, and the EAP counselor to join her in analyzing the situation. She then met with the abused employee, her friend, and her supervisor to report on the team's recommendations.

EAP Counselor: arranged for the abused woman to see another counselor, who had an open appointment that same day for counseling and referral to the community agencies that could help her. The counselor also referred her to a comprehensive shelter for victims of abuse. She explained the comprehensive services the shelter could offer her:

- A safe place to stay with her children;
- Advice on how to get out of her home situation safely;
- Legal advice; and
- Additional helpful information.

Abused Woman: was afraid to change the status quo. After several meetings with the EAP counselor and encouraging talks with her friend, she agreed to talk with the shelter staff. Her friend/co-worker drove her to the meeting. They worked with her to develop a safe plan for leaving home with her children. She also asked the workplace violence team to coordinate with the shelter staff.

Security Director and Supervisor: identified the period immediately after she left home would be a high risk period and arranged for a guard to be at the workplace during that time. Photographs of the husband were supplied to the guard force. With the woman's consent, both the supervisor and security director discussed the situation with co-workers, shared the picture with them, and explained what they should do in various contingencies. At the meeting one coworker began complaining about the danger to her. The friend argued persuasively, *this could happen to any of us. Would you rather we stick together, or leave one another to suffer alone?* This rallied the group, and the co-worker decided to go along with the others.

The supervisor agreed to use flextime and flexi-place options to make the employee more difficult to find. Not only would she be working a different schedule, but she would also report to a suburban telecommuting center instead of the agency's central office.

The supervisor explained to the employee that she would like very much to have her on board full time, as she was an excellent worker, but there was no position available. However, she encouraged her to seek a full time job and made phone calls to colleagues in other departments to develop job leads for her. One of her professional associates offered to allow the employee to use their organization's career transition center that had excellent job search resources and was located in a different part of town from her normal worksite.

7.4.3. Resolution

The employee executed her plan for leaving home and moved to the shelter with her children. She worked with an attorney to obtain financial support and to begin divorce proceedings. She often had times of doubt and fear but found the shelter staff very supportive. Her co-workers encouraged her to call daily with reports on her progress.

The husband appeared at the office only once, a few days after his wife moved into the shelter. He shouted threats at the security guard, who calmly called for back-up from the local police. Fearing for his reputation, he fled the scene before police could arrive. The guard force continued to monitor any efforts by the husband to gain entry to the building.

Six months later, the employee obtained a full-time position at a nearby office within the same agency. She discovered they also had a workplace violence team and made them aware of her situation, just in case she should need their help. She and her children moved into an apartment. At the recommendation of the EAP counselor, the children began seeing a child psychologist to help them make sense of an upsetting situation, and she began attending a support group for battered women. Her friend from her former office helped her with encouragement, support, and suggestions on how to handle the stresses of single parenthood.

7.4.4. Questions for the Agency Planning Group

1) Are your team members knowledgeable about domestic violence?
2) What do you think about the role of the friend? How would you encourage agency employees to support co-workers in these types of situations?
3) Does your agency have access to career transition services to help in these types of situations?
4) Has your planning group identified someone knowledgeable about restraining/protective orders to discuss with the employee the pros and cons of obtaining one?

7.5. Case Study 3: Threat

7.5.1. Incident

When on a break with one of his colleagues from down the hall, an employee was reported to have said,

"I like the way some employees handle problems with their supervisors: they eliminate them. One of these days I'm going to bring in my gun and take care of my problem."

The employee who heard the statement reported it to his supervisor, who in turn reported it to his supervisor, who then called a member of the workplace violence team.

7.5.2. Response

In the case of a reported threat where there does not appear to be an imminent danger, the agency's plan called for the employee relations specialist to conduct an immediate preliminary investigation and for the team to meet with the supervisor immediately afterward to look at the available evidence and strategize a preliminary response.

Employee Relations Specialist: interviewed the employee who heard the threat, that employee's supervisor, the supervisor of the employee who made the threat, and subsequently the employee who allegedly made the threat. The employee who made the threat denied saying any such thing. There were no other witnesses.

Supervisor (of the employee who allegedly made the threat): reported that, several months earlier, the same employee had responded to his casual question about weekend plans by saying, "I'm going to spend the weekend in my basement with my guns practicing my revenge." At that time, the supervisor had warned the employee that such talk was unacceptable at work and referred the employee to EAP. Both supervisors expressed concern for their staff's safety. Based on comments from supervisors and the employee who made the threat, the employee relations specialist recommended that a more thorough investigation be done.

Follow-up Meeting: findings were discussed, and the following people were present:

- First-level supervisor of the employee who allegedly made the threat;
- Second-level supervisor of the employee who allegedly made the threat;
- Associate director of the agency;
- Agency security officer;
- Employee relations specialist;
- EAP counselor; and
- Attorney with the OGC

One of the team members recommended the employee be given a counseling memo and referred to EAP. However, the consensus of the others, based on the employee relations specialist's oral report, was to recommend to the supervisor that the employee be placed on excused absence pending an investigation and that he be escorted from the premises.

Security and the Employee's Second-level Supervisor: went together to give the employee a letter that stated, "This is to inform you that effective immediately, you will be placed on paid, non-duty status pending an agency determination regarding your actions. You are required to provide a phone number where you can be reached during working hours." They also took away his identification badge and office keys and escorted him to the building exit.

OIG and Legal Investigation: OIG arranged for a criminal investigation to be conducted. The criminal investigator interviewed all of the employee's co-workers and two other employees who the co-workers indicated had knowledge of this employee's prior statements about his supervisors. He then interviewed the suspended employee.

The criminal investigator checked to see if the employee had a police record; he did not. The investigator also checked his workplace to see if he had any weapons at the office or if he had any written material of a threatening nature. The search of his workplace found nothing of consequence.

The investigative report showed that the employee told his co-workers on several occasions that he had no respect for his supervisor, and that he thought that threatening him was an effective way to solve his problems with him. Signed witness statements indicated that he bragged about knowing how to get his way with his boss.

The prosecutor's office, after receiving the investigative report, made a determination that it would not prosecute the case and informed management that they could precede with administrative action. The team recommended a proposed removal action since the evidence showed that the employee was using threats to intimidate his supervisor.

7.5.3. Resolution

The second-level supervisor proposed a removal action based on a charge of "threatening a supervisor." A top manager who was not directly involved in the case initially insisted that the agency enter into a settlement agreement that would give the employee a clean SF—50. Based on the particular facts in this case, the team convinced him that he would not be solving any problems by settling the case in this way and would be, in fact, just transferring the problem to another unsuspecting employer. The top manager finally agreed and the employee was removed from Federal service. Even though the agency did not settle the case and did, in fact, effect a removal action, the employee was soon hired by another agency.

> The new agency never checked his references and began experiencing the same type of intimidating behavior from the employee.

7.5.4. Questions for the Agency Planning Group

1) What would your agency have done about checking references before hiring this employee?
2) What do you think would have been the risks of settling the case with a clean SF—50?
3) How would your agency have handled the case if the key witness (i.e., the employee who heard the threat) had demonstrated certain behavior that cast doubt on his credibility?

7.6. Case Study 4: Veiled Threats

7.6.1. Incident

A workplace violence team member took a phone call from a supervisor who said, "One of my employees said this morning that he knows where my kids go to school. I know this may not sound like much, but if you saw the look in his eyes and heard the anger in his voice, you'd know why I need your help in figuring out what to do."

7.6.2. Response

Team Member: who took the call heard more details about the incident and then set up a meeting with the supervisor who made the call, a security specialist, an employee relations specialist, and an EAP counselor.

Supervisor: told the team that the employee in question engaged in intimidating behavior toward him for a year since becoming his supervisor. The supervisor spoke with him on several occasions to let him know that his behavior was unacceptable. He also gave the employee a written warning along with a written referral to the EAP.

Federal Protective Service (FPS) and Law Enforcement: Because the office was in a General Services Administration controlled building, the security specialist called the regional FPS office. FPS contacted the threat assessment unit of the state police, who agreed to assign a threat assessment consultant to assist the agency. In a phone consultation with the team, the threat assessment consultant suggested the team arrange for an immediate investigation by an investigator who was experienced in workplace violence cases. The investigator should explore the following areas:

1) What further background information could be learned about the relationship between the supervisor and employee?
2) What was the relationship between the supervisor and his other employees and coworkers?
3) Was there evidence of problems of a similar nature with the employee's previous supervisors? If so, how were they resolved or handled? If there were problems with previous supervisors, were they similar to or different from the current situation?
4) What were the alleged employee's relationships with co-workers? Might there have been other potential victims? Were there also interpersonal problems between the employee and other employees?

5) Were there unusually stressful problems in the life of the employee (e.g., divorce, financial reversal, or any other recent significant traumatic event)?
6) Did anyone else feel threatened based on their interaction with the employee?
7) Did the employee have access to weapons? Had he recently acquired weapons?

The threat assessment consultant scheduled another telephone consultation with the team for three days later. He also suggested the investigator refrain from interviewing the alleged perpetrator until after the next phone consultation.

Legal Investigation and Threat Assessment Team: was conducted immediately by a professional investigator and the team reviewed the investigative report prior to the next phone conversation with the threat assessment consultant. The report contained statements by the employee's supervisor about veiled threats the employee had made, such as, "If you give me that assignment, you'll be sorry. I know where you live, and I see you every day on your way to work." Also, the employee lived at the opposite end of town from the supervisor.

The investigative report included a transcript and a tape recording of two voicemail messages that the supervisor found intimidating: one in which the employee said he needed annual leave that day to go for target practice, and another where the employee said he could not come to work that day because he had to go hunting. Again, the supervisor's statement showed he considered the employee's tone of voice to be intimidating and said, on the day previous to each of these phone calls, the employee acted as though he was angry about new assignments the supervisor gave him. The supervisor said he took several precautions as a result of the threats.

For example, he told his children to take precautions, installed dead bolt locks at his home, and asked the local police to do a security survey of his home. In addition to the investigative report, the security office obtained a police record on the employee showing a misdemeanor conviction for spousal abuse several years earlier.

Participating in the phone consultation with the threat assessment consultant was the workplace violence team, the second-line supervisor, and the director of the office. The purpose of the consultation was to:

- Analyze the information contained in the investigative report;
- Determine what additional information was needed;
- Determine whether to interview the alleged perpetrator;
- Help the team members organize their thinking about how to proceed with the case; and
- Discuss a range of options that could be taken.

The threat assessment consultant recommended the investigator interview three co-workers, the employee's ex-wife, and subsequently the employee. The purpose of the interview with the employee would be to corroborate what was said by the others and get his explanation of why he made the statements. The interviewer would also communicate to him that this kind of conduct had been noticed, troubled people, and was not condoned. The consultant recommended additional security measures for the interview, including having a security officer in the next room. The threat assessment consultant also gave the team guidance in the preservation of evidence such as written materials, tape recordings, and documentation of all contacts.

During the interview, the employee made what the investigator believed were several additional veiled threats against the supervisor. He even behaved in a way that led the investigator to be concerned about his own safety.

Based on the findings of the investigation, the threat assessment consultant concluded the employee presented a real possibility of carrying out some of the threats toward the supervisor’s family. He expressed concern the situation could escalate if the employee continued to work in the same office. Management decided to place the employee on excused absence for the safety of the threatened supervisor.

The threat assessment consultant worked with team members to develop a plan for ongoing security. For example, he suggested the team identify one member to coordinate case management, recommended monitoring any further communication between the employee and other agency employees (e.g., phone calls, e-mail messages, and any sighting at residences were to be reported to the case manager). He recommended security officials be in the area, though not visible, whenever meetings were held with the employee. The threat assessment consultant remained available for telephone consultation as the team carried out the plan.

7.6.3. Resolution

Though the agency had concerns that any agency action might trigger retaliation against the supervisor's family, the agency went ahead and removed the employee based on a charge of threatening behavior. The agency's analysis considered the credibility of the supervisor, employee, and the information and evidence gathered. The employee did not appeal the removal action.

The agency security officer gave the supervisor advice on personal safety and discussed with him the pros and cons of obtaining a restraining order for his family. The security officer also helped the supervisor get in touch with the local office of victim assistance for additional ideas on ways to protect his family. The threat assessment consultant also spoke with the supervisor and suggested he may want to go to the school, school bus driver, and neighbors and make them aware of the problem and the employee's appearance (show them his picture). The reason for involving the school and neighbors would be to encourage them to report any suspicious activities to the police. The security officer talked to the supervisor about police involvement and discussed filing criminal charges. If the police said the situation was not serious enough to file criminal charges, he suggested finding out from the police what actions would warrant an arrest. For example, the supervisor could discuss with police a pattern of behavior that might be considered serious enough to pursue action under the state's stalking or harassment statute.

7.6.4. Questions for the Agency Planning Group

1) If this incident were reported at your agency, would you have used a criminal investigator or administrative investigator to conduct the initial investigation?
2) If your agency has a criminal investigative service, have you discussed the feasibility of involving agency criminal investigators at an early stage in the process of dealing with threatening behavior (i.e., in situations where threatening behavior does not yet rise to the level of a crime)?
3) Has your agency identified a threat assessment professional to whom you could turn for assistance if the need arose?
4) How does your agency keep up with Merit Systems Protection Board case law on charges and threats?
5) If this happened at your agency, and the threatening behavior continued, what would you do to protect the supervisor and his family?

7.7. Case Study 5: Threat

7.7.1. Incident

A visibly upset male employee cornered a female employee in her office. Quietly and slowly he said she would pay with her life for going over his head to ask about his work. The male employee then stared at his co-worker with his hands clenched rigidly at his side before leaving the office and slamming the door behind him. The female employee, fearful and shaken, reported this to her supervisor, who immediately reported the incident to the Director of Employee Relations.

7.7.2. Response

The agency's response plan called for involvement of employee relations, security, and EAP in cases involving threats. Immediately following the report to the response team, the security officer contacted the female employee to assist her in filing a police report on the threat and to discuss safety measures she should take. The victim was also referred to EAP, where she received brief counseling and educational materials on handling severe stress.

An investigation was immediately conducted by OIG. In her statement, the female employee repeated what she reported to the supervisor earlier about the threat. In his statement, the male employee stated that, on the day in question, he was upset about what he felt were some underhanded activities by the female employee, and his only recollection about the conversation was that he made a general statement to her like "You'll pay." He stated this was not a threat, but just an expression. The investigation showed the employee had several previous incidents of intimidating behavior that resulted in disciplinary actions.

7.7.3. Resolution

After reviewing the results of the investigation, the supervisor proposed a removal action, finding the female employee's version of the incident more credible. In his response to the proposed notice, the employee brought in medical documentation that said he had a psychiatric disability of post-traumatic stress disorder causing his misconduct, and he requested a reasonable accommodation. The deciding official consulted with an agency attorney and employee relations specialist who explained that nothing in the Rehabilitation Act prohibits an agency from maintaining a workplace free of violence or threats of violence. Further, they explained a request for reasonable accommodation does not excuse employee misconduct nor does it shield an employee from discipline. The deciding official determined removal was the appropriate discipline in this case. The employee did not appeal the action.

7.7.4. Questions for the Agency Planning Group

1) Do you agree with the agency's approach in this case?
2) If this situation occurred at your agency, would you have involved law enforcement in the process?
3) Who would conduct the investigation at your agency?
4) What else would your agency have done to protect the employee?
5) Would you have requested more medical documentation from the employee?
6) What risks must be balanced when selecting a penalty?

7.8. Case Study 6: Threat Made during an EAP Counseling Session

7.8.1. Incident

When the employee first contacted the in-house EAP counselor several months earlier, he said he was referred by his supervisor because of frequent tardiness and his inability to complete assignments on time. He complained of lack of interest in his job and inability to sleep. The counselor referred the employee to a psychiatrist for evaluation. The employee agreed to sign releases so the counselor could contact both his supervisor and the psychiatrist. The psychiatrist diagnosed depression, prescribed an anti-depressant, and referred the employee for psychotherapy.

Several weeks later, the supervisor called the EAP counselor to report that the employee often came in looking disheveled; co-workers complained his speech and manner were sometimes bizarre; and he bragged of drinking large amounts of alcohol each evening. The counselor immediately called the employee and asked him to come in for a follow-up visit. He agreed and appeared late that afternoon in a euphoric state. He said he never felt better in his life and decided against psychotherapy. The counselor encouraged him to return to the psychiatrist for reevaluation, but the employee refused.

The employee was in a talkative mood and began to reminisce about his Federal career: first his early successes, then recent disappointments such as being passed over repeatedly for promotions and failure to receive any type of recognition. As he continued, he revealed in a matter-of-fact tone he had been spending his evenings planning revenge on his managers, because they had treated him unfairly for many years and deserved to be punished. He believed he had planned the "perfect murder" and that he would never be caught. Thinking that he was venting frustrations, the counselor questioned the employee further and quickly realized he was very serious. She urged him to call his psychiatrist immediately, and he again refused but said he would "think about calling" in a day or two.

7.8.2. Response

As soon as the employee left the EAP counselor's office, the counselor called the psychiatrist and asked whether he viewed the employee's statement as a threat. The psychiatrist said he believed it was a serious threat and recommended immediate action be taken. The EAP counselor called the police and agency officials and informed them about the situation. The following morning when the employee reported to the office, he was met by the local police. A police officer brought him to the community's emergency services clinic for an evaluation and subsequently transported him to the hospital. He remained in the hospital for several weeks.

7.8.3. Resolution

Following discharge from the hospital, the employee remained at home for several more weeks, during which time agency management held many discussions with his treating and consulting physicians. It was finally decided and agreed upon by the team that the employee would be allowed to return to work and not be removed from his position on the following conditions as long as he remained an employee of the agency:

- Continue in psychotherapy;
- Remain on medication as prescribed;
- Refrain from alcohol and other drug abuse; and
- Be seen on a regular basis by a psychiatric consultant to the agency.

Although co-workers were concerned about the employee's strange behavior and saw him removed from the premises by the police, several visited him in the hospital and were supportive of his return to the office. He worked his remaining years with no further problems, then retired and moved to another state.

7.8.4. Questions for the Agency Planning Group

1) Do you agree with the agency's approach in handling this case?
2) Would you have let the employee back to work after his hospitalization?
3) What information would you need to make this determination?
4) What safety precautions would your agency take if you did/did not take him back?
5) What should the EAP counselor have done if the employee denied making the threat?
6) Would your agency have proposed disciplinary action prior to the last chance agreement?

7.9. Case Study 7: Threats Made by a Former Employee

7.9.1. Incident

The first incident report that came into the agency's newly formed workplace violence team was from a field office. Two months after an employee retired on disability retirement, he began threatening his former supervisor. He knocked on his former supervisor's apartment door late one evening. He left threatening statements on the supervisor's home answering machine such as, "I just wanted to let you know I bought a gun." On one occasion, a psychiatrist called the supervisor as well as the agency's security office and told them that the former employee threatened to murder him. The psychiatrist said the threat should be taken seriously especially due to the heavy drinking of the former employee. A co-worker received an anonymous letter stating, "It is not over with [name of supervisor]." Each time a threat was reported, the agency's security office would take extra measures to protect the supervisor while at the workplace, and the supervisor would report the incident to the local police. Each time, the supervisor was informed that the police were unable to take action on the threats because they did not rise to a criminal level. The supervisor spoke with the county magistrate about a restraining order; however, once again, was told the threats did not rise to the level required to obtain a restraining order.

7.9.2. Response

The workplace violence team held a conference call with the security officer, director of the office, the supervisor, and the security chief of the field office. Roles were discussed and each person was informed they should perform their allotted actions.

Security Officer:

- Confirmed the whereabouts of the former employee and periodically reconfirmed his whereabouts;
- Met with local police to determine whether the former employee's behavior constituted a crime in the jurisdiction and whether other applicable charges (e.g., stalking or harassment) might be considered;
- Asked if the police department had a threat assessment unit or access to one at the state level;
- Asked police about contacting the U. S. Postal Service for assistance in tracing the anonymous letter (18 U.S.C. §876);
- Met with the psychiatrist who called the agency, and asked him to send a letter to the chief of police reporting the threats;
- Informed the psychiatrist about the former employee's behavior and discussed whether or not involuntary hospitalization might be an option;
- Attempted to establish an ongoing dialogue with the psychiatrist and tried to get a commitment to share information about the case to the extent allowed by confidentiality; Provided periodic updates to the supervisor on the status of the case, actions taken, and actions being contemplated; and
- Provided support and advice to the supervisor including telephone numbers and points of contact for the local telephone company, local law enforcement, and local victim assistance organizations.

Director of the Field Office:

- Met with security and police to consider options (and their ramifications) for encouraging the former employee to cease and abstain from his threatening activities; and
- Provided support to the supervisor by encouraging the supervisor to utilize the Employee Assistance Program.

Supervisor:

- Kept detailed notes about each contact with the former employee;
- Gave copies of all the notes to the police. (They explained to the supervisor that in all
- probability, each time he went to the police, it was treated like a new report, and thus, as
- individual incidents, they had not risen to the level of a crime.);
- Contacted the phone company to alert them to the situation;
- Tape recorded all messages left on the answering machine; and
- Contacted the local office of victim assistance for additional ideas.

7.9.3. Resolution

Contact with the local police confirmed each report was treated as a new case. When presented with the cumulative evidence, in fact, the former employee's behavior did rise to the level of stalking under state law. The police visited the former employee and warned him that further threats could result in an arrest. At the supervisor's request, the county magistrate issued a restraining order prohibiting personal contact and any communication. Two months after the restraining order was issued, the former employee was arrested for breaking the restraining order. The agency security office and the supervisor kept in contact with the police about the case to reduce any further risk of violence.

7.9.4. Questions for the Agency Planning Group

1) Do you think the agency's approach in this case was adequate protect the supervisor?
2) Have you already established liaison with appropriate law enforcement authorities to ensure that situations such as this get the proper attention from the beginning?
3) What would your agency do if the psychiatrist refused to get involved? Are there any laws in your state requiring mental health professionals to protect potential victims when threats have been made?
4) How would you continue to monitor the former employee's activities after he is released from jail?
5) What would your agency do if the case continued without the former employee being arrested?

7.10. Case Study 8: Threats from Non-Employees

7.10.1. Incident

The agency's new workplace violence team received a call from a small field office. The field office staff consisted of three employees, two of whom spent much of their workday outside of the office. All three employees had close calls in the past in dealing with violent individuals. On two occasions, clients who came into the office lost their tempers because they received answers they did not like. Several times the employees who conducted their business outside the office were the targets of threats and aggressive behavior. "How can you help us out here in the field?" they asked the workplace violence team.

7.10.2. Response

Presented with this problem, the workplace violence team consulted with the following organizations:

- Local law enforcement agency in the jurisdiction where the field office was located; Several Federal law enforcement agencies, including FPS;
- Other Federal government agencies that had small field offices and workers in the field; The National Center for Victims of Crime; and
- State police prevention units located near the agency field offices.

7.10.3. Resolution

The agency implemented the following plan not only for the office that made the initial request, but for many of their other field offices as well.

- Install a panic button connected to a security service in the office ;
- Install a video camera (with an audio component) in the public service area;
- Reconfigure office furniture, especially in public service areas, to maximize security;
- Train all employees in personal safety techniques;
- Provide back-up for employees in the field when a threatening situation is suspected;
- Provide copies of the laws regarding harassment, threats, and stalking in their states;

- Provide lists of state and local organizations that can assist in preventing violence;
- Develop and maintain liaison with state and local law enforcement agencies;
- Establish a system of daily, periodic check-ins for employees in the field; and
- Provide cellular phones, personal alarms, and other safety devices as appropriate.

7.10.4. Questions for the Agency Planning Group

1) Do you agree with the agency's approach in this case?
2) What more could be done?

7.11. Case Study 9: Intimidation without Previous Behavior

7.11.1. Incident

A supervisor reported to a human resources (HR) specialist that one of his employees (alleged victim) recently stated another employee (alleged perpetrator) was intimidating him with "in your face" behavior. The alleged perpetrator engaged in several intimidating behaviors: standing over the alleged victim's desk in what was perceived as menacing, physically crowded the victim out of an elevator, and making menacing gestures. The supervisor stated the alleged perpetrator was an average performer, somewhat of a loner, but there were no behavior problems the supervisor was aware of until the employee came to him expressing fear. The supervisor said the reporting employee did not want the supervisor to say anything to anyone, so the supervisor observed the situation for a couple of days. When he did not observe any of the behaviors described, he spoke with the alleged victim again and told him he would consult with the crisis management team.

7.11.2. Response

In cases involving reports of intimidation, this agency's crisis response plan called for involvement of HR and EAP (with the clear understanding the agency would contact other resources as needed). The HR specialist’s first action was to set up a meeting for the next day with the supervisor, an EAP counselor, and another HR specialist who was skilled in conflict resolution.

Several options were discussed at that meeting. One was to initiate an immediate investigation into the allegations that involved interviewing the alleged victim, any witnesses identified by the alleged victim, and the alleged perpetrator. Another suggestion offered by the EAP counselor was that, in view of the alleged victim's reluctance to speak up about the incident, they could arrange a training session for the entire office on conflict resolution that would allow the EAP counselor to observe the dynamics of the entire work group. The EAP counselor noted conflict resolution classes were regularly scheduled at the agency. The supervisor also admitted he was aware of a lot of tensions in the office and would like EAP's assistance in resolving whatever was causing them.

After discussing the options, the supervisor and the team decided to try the conflict resolution training session before initiating an investigation. At the training session, during some of the exercises, it became clear the alleged victim not only contributed significantly to the conflicts and tension with the alleged perpetrator, but also with other employees and in the office in general. The alleged perpetrator seemed to react assertively, but not inappropriately, to the alleged victim's attempts to annoy him.

7.11.3. Resolution

Office tensions were reduced to minimum as a result of the training session and follow-up work by EAP. The employee who initially reported the intimidation to his supervisor not only realized what he was doing to contribute to office tensions, but he also actively sought help to change his approach and began to conduct himself more effectively with his co-workers. He appreciated getting the situation resolved in a low-key way that did not cause him embarrassment and began to work cooperatively with the alleged perpetrator. The alleged perpetrator never learned about the original complaint, but he did learn from the training session more effective ways to conduct himself with his co-workers. The agency reported that both employees became productive team players.

7.11.4. Questions for the Agency Planning Group

1) Do you agree with the agency's approach in this situation?
2) Can you think of other situations that could be addressed effectively through an intervention with the work group?
3) In what kinds of situations would this approach be counter-productive?
4) Can you envision a scenario where using the group conflict resolution session to get at any individualized problem might have a negative, rather than a positive, effect?

5) Has your agency conducted employee training on such topics as conflict resolution, stress management, and dealing with hostile persons?

7.12. Case Study 10: Intimidation with Previous Behavior

7.12.1. Incident

An employee called a member of the agency crisis team for advice, saying that a co-worker was picking on her and expressing fear that something serious might happen. For several weeks, a coworker had been making statements such as, "You actually took credit for my work and you're spreading rumors that I'm no good. If you ever get credit for my work again, that will be the last time you take credit for anybody's work. I'll make sure of that." She also said her computer files had been altered on several occasions and she suspected it was the same co-worker. When she reported the situation to her supervisor, he tried to convince her there was no real danger and she was blowing things out of proportion; however, she continued to worry. She said she spoke with her union representative who suggested she contact the agency's workplace violence team.

7.12.2. Response

The agency's plan called for the initial involvement of employee relations and EAP in situations involving intimidation. The employee relations specialist and the EAP counselor met with the supervisor of the employee who reported the incident.

Supervisor: told the employee relations specialist and the EAP counselor he was aware of the situation, but the woman who reported it tended to exaggerate. He knew the alleged perpetrator well as he had supervised him for years, stating: "He just talks that way; he's not really dangerous." He gave examples of how the alleged perpetrator is all talk and not likely to act out. One example occurred several months earlier when he talked to the alleged perpetrator about his poor performance. The employee became agitated and accused the supervisor of being unfair, siding with the other employees, and believing the rumors the co-workers were spreading about him. He stood up and in an angry voice said, "You better start treating me fairly or you're going to be the one with the problem." The supervisor reasoned that, since he had always been that way, the employee was not a real threat to anyone.

During the initial meeting, the team asked the supervisor to sign a written statement about these incidents and recommended he take disciplinary action. However, the supervisor was reluctant to sign a statement or to initiate disciplinary action and could not be persuaded by their recommendations to do so.

Employee Relations Specialist: conducted an investigation. Interviews with other co-workers confirmed the intimidating behavior on the part of the alleged perpetrator and several co-workers said they felt threatened by him. None were willing to sign affidavits. The investigator also found a witness to the incident where the supervisor was threatened. As the alleged perpetrator left the supervisor's office and passed by the secretary's desk, he said, "He's an (expletive) and he better watch himself." However, the secretary was also unwilling to sign an affidavit.

After confirming the validity of the allegations, but with the supervisor refusing to take action and the only affidavit being from the employee who originally reported the situation, the team considered courses of action:

- Arrange for the reassignment of the victim to a less threatening work situation;
- Report the situation to the second-line supervisor;
- Recommend the second-line supervisor propose disciplinary action against the alleged perpetrator; and
- Locate an investigator with experience in workplace violence cases.

Legal Investigation: the investigator would conduct interviews with the reluctant witnesses and be given a letter of authorization from the director of the office stating the requirement that employees must cooperate in the investigation or face disciplinary action.

The team located an investigator who was experienced in workplace violence cases from a nearby Federal agency and worked out an interagency agreement to obtain his services. During the investigation, he showed the letter of authorization to only one employee and to the supervisor as he was able to persuade the others to sign written affidavits without resorting to showing them the letter. The results of the investigation showed evidence of intimidating behavior by the alleged perpetrator.

The agency security specialist met with the alleged perpetrator to inform him to have no further contact with the victim. He also met with the victim to give her advice on how to handle a situation like this if it were to happen again. In addition, he recommended a procedure to the team that would monitor computer use in the division.

This action resulted in evidence showing that the employee was, in fact, altering computer files.

7.12.3. Resolution

The first-line supervisor was given a written reprimand by the second-line supervisor for failing to take proper action in a timely manner and for failing to ensure a safe work environment. He was counseled about the poor performance of his supervisory duties. The alleged perpetrator was charged with both disruptive behavior and gaining malicious access to a non-authorized computer. Based on this information, he was removed from Federal service.

7.12.4. Questions for the Agency Planning Group

1. Would supervisory training likely have resulted in quicker action against the alleged perpetrator?
2. Do you have other approaches for convincing a recalcitrant supervisor to take action?
3. Do you have other approaches for convincing reluctant witnesses to give written statements?
4. Are you up-to-date on the case law associated with requiring the subject of an investigation to give statements?
5. If you had not been able to convince the reluctant witnesses to give written statements, and you only had the one affidavit to support the one incident, do you think this would have provided your agency with enough evidence to take disciplinary action? If so, what type of penalty would likely be given in this case?

7.13. Case Study 11: Frightening Behavior Due to Personal Problems

7.13.1. Incident

A supervisor contacted the Employee Relations Office because one of his employees was making the other employees in the office uncomfortable. He said the employee did not seem engaged in any actionable misconduct. However, due to the agency's new workplace violence policy and training he had received, he thought he should at least mention the situation. The employee was recently divorced and went through a difficult time for over two years. He also made it clear he was having financial problems that caused him to be more stressed. He was irritable and aggressive in his speech much of the time. He would routinely talk about the number of guns he owned in general conversation where he would mention someone else was causing all of his problems.

7.13.2. Response

At the first meeting with the supervisor, the employee relations specialist and the EAP counselor suggested that, since this was a long-running situation rather than an immediate crisis, the supervisor had time to do some fact-finding. They gave him several suggestions on what to do while safeguarding the privacy of the employee (e.g., request a confidential conversation with previous supervisors, go back for more information to co-workers who registered complaints, and review his personnel records). Two days later they had another meeting to discuss the case and strategize a plan of action.

The supervisor's initial fact-finding showed the employee's co-workers attributed his aggressive behavior to the difficult divorce situation; however, they were afraid of him. The supervisor did not learn any more specifics about why they were afraid, except that he was short-tempered, ill-mannered, and spoke a lot about his guns. Although, according to the co-workers, he spoke of his guns in a matter-of-fact rather than in an intimidating manner.

After getting ideas from the employee relations specialist and the EAP counselor, the supervisor sat down with the employee and discussed his behavior. He told the employee his peers were uncomfortable and that it must stop. He referred the employee to EAP, setting a time and date to meet with the counselor.

7.13.3. Resolution

As a result of counseling by the supervisor and by the EAP counselor, the employee changed his behavior. He was unaware his behavior was scaring people. He learned new ways from EAP to interact with people. EAP referred him to a therapist in the community to address underlying personal problems. The supervisor continued to monitor the employee's conduct.

7.13.4. Questions for the Agency Planning Group

1) Do you agree with the agency's approach in this case?
2) Can you think of other situations that would lend themselves to this kind of low-key approach?

3) Does your agency have effective EAP training so that supervisors are comfortable in turning to the EAP for advice?

7.14. Case Study 12: Frightening Behavior Due to Mental Conditions

7.14.1. Incident

Several employees in an office went to their supervisor to report an unusual situation that occurred the previous day. An agency employee from a different building was seen going in and out of their office over a seven-hour period. She remarked to several people "the government" kept her prisoner, inserted microphones in her head to hear what she was thinking, and tampered with her computer to feed her evil thoughts. She also said her doctors diagnosed her as paranoid schizophrenic, but that they are wrong about her. She made inflammatory remarks about coworkers, and made threatening statements such as, “Anyone in my old job who got in my way came down with mysterious illnesses.”

7.14.2. Response

Employee Relations Specialist: immediately informed the employee's supervisor about the incident. She learned from the employee's supervisor the employee performed adequately until a few months ago, but had always seemed withdrawn and eccentric. However, her behavior had changed. She often roamed around the office, spending an hour or more with any employee she could corner. It was later learned she had stopped taking her medication. Several employees reported to the supervisor they were afraid she might hurt them because of her inflammatory statements. She also learned a former supervisor previously gave the employee a reprimand and two counseling memoranda for inappropriate language and absence from the worksite in addition to offering her leave for treatment as a reasonable accommodation.

Upon the recommendation of the employee relations specialist, the employee was placed on excused absence pending further agency inquiry and response with a requirement to call in daily. The employee relations specialist, a trained investigator, conducted interviews with the employees who filed the reports and with the employee's co-workers. She found most of the employees were afraid of the woman because of her inflammatory statements.

The employee relations specialist then set up a meeting with the woman's first-and second-line supervisor, the director of personnel, legal office, director of security, the agency's medical officer, and EAP counselor. The following options were raised:

- Propose an indefinite suspension pending an investigation (option rejected because the agency already had all the information it needed about the incident);
- Reassign or demote the employee to another office (option rejected because the reported conduct was too serious);
- Propose a suspension based on her day-long frightening and disruptive comments and conduct (option rejected because the reported conduct was too serious);
- Order a medical examination to determine whether the employee was fit for duty (option rejected because the employee was not in a position with medical standards or physical requirements);
- Offer a medical examination (option rejected because supervisor already tried it several times); and
- Offer her leave for treatment (option rejected because supervisor already tried it).

The Team: recommended the supervisor issue a proposal to remove based on the events in the other office (e.g. her day-long frightening, disruptive comments and conduct). They suggested the notice also refer to the earlier counseling memos and the reprimand that placed the employee on notice concerning her absence from her office and inappropriate behavior.

The supervisor proposed her removal. Three weeks later, the employee and her brother-in-law came in for her oral reply to the proposed notice. She denied making any of the statements attributed to her. Her brother-in-law asked the deciding official to order her to go for a psychiatric examination, but he was told that regulations prohibited the agency from doing so. The employee did not provide any additional medical documentation.

7.14.3. Resolution

The agency proceeded with a removal action based on her disruptive behavior. Once her brother-in-law realized her salary and health benefits would soon cease, he was able to convince her to go to the hospital for the help she needed and to file for disability retirement. The agency assisted her in filing forms with OPM. The disability retirement was approved by OPM and this provided her with income and a continuation of medical coverage.

7.14.4. Questions for the Agency Planning Group

1) Do you agree with the agency's approach in handling this case?
2) Does your employee training direct employees to call security or 911 in emergency situations?
3) Is your team knowledgeable about accessing appropriate community resources for emergency situations?
4) What if the employee had not been willing and able to apply for disability retirement herself? Do you know the rules (discussed in PART II: Section 3) concerning the agency's filing for disability retirement on behalf of the employee?
5) Does your agency's supervisory training encourage early intervention in cases of this type?

7.15. Case Study 13: Disruptive Behavior

7.15.1. Incident

An employee called the EAP member of the workplace violence team for advice on dealing with his senior co-worker. The agency recently provided workplace violence training that emphasized early intervention. He said a co-worker hired at the GS-14 level six months earlier was in the habit of shouting and making demeaning remarks to the other employees in the office. The senior co-worker was skilled in twisting words and manipulating situations to his advantage. For example, when employees would ask him for advice on a topic in his area of expertise, he would tell them to use their own common sense. Then when they finished the assignment, he would make demeaning remarks about them and speak loudly about how they incorrectly completed their work. At other times, he would rudely and loudly demand they drop whatever they were working on and help him with his project. The employee said he had attempted to speak with his supervisor about the situation, but was told "not to make a mountain out of a mole hill."

7.15.2. Response

EAP Counselor: met with the employee who reported the situation. The employee described feelings of being overwhelmed and helpless. The demeaning remarks were becoming intolerable. The employee believed attempts to resolve the issue with the co-worker were futile. The fact the supervisor minimized the situation further discouraged the employee. However, by the end of the meeting with the counselor, the employee was able to recognize that not saying anything was not helping and was actually allowing a bad situation to get worse.

At a subsequent meeting, the EAP counselor and the employee explored skills to address the situation in a respectful, reasonable, and responsible manner with both his supervisor and coworker. The counselor suggested using language such as:

- I do not like shouting and please lower your voice;
- I do not like it when you put me down in front of my peers;
- It is demeaning when I am told that I am...;
- I do not like it when you point your finger at me; and
- I want to have a good working relationship with you.

The Employee: learned to focus on his personal professionalism and responsibility to establish and maintain reasonable boundaries and limits by using these types of firm and friendly "I statements." This allowed him to acknowledge he heard and understood what the supervisor and co-worker were saying, and repeating what he needed to communicate to them.

After practicing with the EAP counselor, the employee was able to discuss the situation again with his supervisor. He described the situation in non-blaming terms and expressed his intentions to work at improving the situation. The supervisor acknowledged the shouting was annoying, but again asked the employee not to aggravate the situation. The employee took a deep breath and said, "It may be a mole hill, but it is affecting my ability to get my work done efficiently." Finally, the supervisor stated he did not realize how disruptive the situation had become and agreed to monitor the situation.

The next time the co-worker raised his voice, the employee used his newly acquired assertiveness skills and stated in a calm and quiet voice, "I don't like to be shouted at. Please lower your voice." When the co-worker started shouting again, the employee restated in a calm voice, "I don't like being shouted at. Please lower your voice." The co-worker stormed away.

The Supervisor: began monitoring the situation. He noted the senior co-worker's abusive conduct improved with the newly assertive employee, but continued to be rude and demeaning toward the other employees. The supervisor consulted with the EAP counselor and employee relations specialist. The counselor told him, "Generally, people don't change unless they have a reason to change." The counselor added the reasons people change can range from simple "I statements," such as those suggested above, to disciplinary actions. The employee relations specialist discussed possible disciplinary options with the supervisor.

The supervisor then met with the co-worker who blamed the altercations on the others in the office. The supervisor responded, "I understand the others were stressed. I'm glad you understand that shouting, speaking in a demeaning manner, and rudely ordering people around is unprofessional and disrespectful. It is unacceptable behavior and will not be tolerated." During the meeting, he also referred the employee to EAP.

The co-worker continued his rude and demeaning behavior to the other employees in spite of the supervisor's efforts. The others, after observing the newly acquired confidence and calm of the employee who first raised the issue, requested similar training from EAP. The supervisor met again with the EAP counselor and employee relations specialist to strategize next steps.

7.15.3. Resolution

When all of the employees in the office started using assertive statements, the co-worker became more cooperative. However, it took a written reprimand, a short suspension, and several counseling sessions with the EAP counselor before he ceased his shouting and rude behavior altogether.

7.15.4. Questions for the Agency Planning Group

1) Does your workplace violence training include communication skills to put a stop to disruptive behavior at an stage early (including skills for convincing reluctant supervisors to act)?
2) How would your agency have proceeded with the case if the co-worker had threatened the employee who spoke to him in an assertive way?
3) What recourse would the employee have had if the supervisor had refused to intervene?

7.16. Case Study 14: Threats of a Suicide Attempt

7.16.1. Incident

A member of the agency's Incident Response Team received a frantic call from an employee saying her co-worker just left her office muttering about the final straw: "You all won't have me to push around anymore." She said she worried for weeks about the possibility of her co-worker committing suicide and knew she should have called earlier. The staff member who took the call told the employee to see if she could find her co-worker and remain with her. Help was on its way.

7.16.2. Response

For incidents involving suicide threats, the agency's plan was to call local police if there seemed to be imminent danger. If there is insufficient information about the situation, then there is a need to contact security and the EAP counselor to do an immediate assessment of the situation.

The team member who took the initial call first contacted a security officer, who immediately located the two employees. The EAP counselor could not be reached immediately, so the team member called an employee in the HR department who earlier volunteered to help in emergency situations as she had been trained in her community in dealing with suicide attempts.

HR Specialist: arrived at the distressed employee's office within two minutes of the call. The employee was crying at this point and making statements such as, "No one can help me," and "It'll be over soon." The HR specialist recognized what was happening and asked the security officer to call police and an ambulance and tell them there was a suicide attempt. After calling the police, the security officer went outside to meet the emergency workers and direct them to the scene. The HR specialist then learned from the woman she had swallowed 10 pills an hour earlier. The police and ambulance were on the scene within three minutes of the call and the woman was hospitalized.

The HR specialist contacted the employee's family and then prepared a report of the incident. The EAP counselor consoled and supported the co-worker, who had initially called the Incident Response Team.

Emergency treatment was successful, and the employee was admitted to the hospital's psychiatric unit. The EAP counselor and HR specialist stayed in touch with the employee and supported her in planning her return to work. She returned to work four weeks later, functioning with the help of anti-depressant medication and twice-weekly psychotherapy sessions.

With the employee's consent, the EAP counselor arranged a meeting involving the employee, her supervisor, and the HR specialist to coordinate her treatment and work activities. The supervisor agreed to adjust the employee's work schedule to fit her therapy appointments as a reasonable accommodation and provided guidance on procedures and medical documentation requirements for leave approval. The counselor, supervisor, and employee agreed on a plan for getting the employee emergency help should she feel another crisis coming on.

7.16.3. Resolution

Two years later, the employee was doing well, working a normal schedule, and serving as a productive employee. She no longer took anti-depressant medication, but she stayed in touch with both her psychiatrist and the EAP counselor.

7.16.4. Questions for the Agency Planning Group

1) Do you agree with the agency's approach in this case?
2) Does your agency have alternate plans for situations where key team members are not available?
3) Has your agency identified employees with skills in handling emergencies?
4) Does your workplace violence policy and training encourage employees to report incidents at an early stage?
5) Does your workplace violence policy and training encourage employees to seek guidance with regard to problems that trouble them even when they don't fully understand the nature of the problem?
6) If the employee had left the building before emergency personnel arrived, would your plan have provided for contacting the appropriate authorities?

7.17. Case Study 15: Viciously Beating and Wounding a Co-worker

7.17.1. Incident

The following incident was reported to the agency's Incident Response Team. A female employee broke off a romantic relationship with a male co-worker, but he would not leave her alone. She finally had a restraining order served to him. After receiving the restraining order, the perpetrator lost control and entered the woman's office. He hit her, and she fell from her chair. While she was on the floor, he broke a soda bottle and cut her face with the broken glass. While this was going on, co-workers heard the commotion and called the police. The perpetrator fled the scene before police arrived and the victim was transported to the hospital.

7.17.2. Response

The Incident Response Team immediately took action.

Security: worked with hospital security to ensure the victim received around-the-clock security while she was in the hospital. He ensured that the hospital staff knew not to give out any information about the victim to callers. He gave the victim advice, reading material, and a video on personal safety. He made sure the perpetrator's card key was deactivated and he had pictures of the perpetrator made for the building guards. He coordinated efforts with local police.

EAP: visited the victim in the hospital and ensured she was seen regularly by a social worker on the hospital staff. She worked with the victim's colleagues to help them be supportive of the victim when she came back to work. The EAP counselor visited the worksite to let co-workers know she was available to them.

Employee Relations Specialist: contacted the agency's OGC and OIG and alerted them to the situation so they could begin to monitor any criminal proceedings. He helped the supervisor develop a notice of proposed indefinite suspension using the crime provision set forth in 5 U.S.C. 7513(b).

Union: was fully supportive of the agency's efforts to help the victim. Since both the victim and the perpetrator were bargaining unit employees, the union was aware of its role to represent all employees in the bargaining unit. In this particular case, the perpetrator filed a grievance, but because of the viciousness of the attack, union officials were reluctant to take the case to arbitration. In addition, realizing this could happen to other employees, the union officials obtained brochures on stalking from their national headquarters and invited an expert speaker on the subject to a chapter meeting.

Supervisor: obtained all the necessary forms and assisted the employee in filing an Office of Workers Compensation Programs (OWCP) claim to pay for hospital and medical costs. The supervisor and the employee's co-workers visited her in the hospital, kept in touch with her during her convalescence, and kept her up-to-date on news from the office.

Legal Investigation: An agency attorney maintained contact with the local prosecutor's office.

7.17.3. Resolution

The police caught and arrested the perpetrator after about 10 days. The agency proposed and effected a removal action against the perpetrator based on a charge of "wounding a co-worker." He did not appeal the action.

The employee remained hospitalized for two days and then went to the home of a friend until the perpetrator was apprehended. She remained at home for another two weeks before returning to work. Her OWCP claim was accepted. She continued to stay in touch with the EAP counselor who had visited her at the hospital and assisted her during her time away from the office. The counselor referred her to a support group for battered women, which she found to be very helpful.

The perpetrator was found guilty and received jail time. After jail time was served, and at the suggestion of an agency attorney, the court forbade the perpetrator to contact the victim or the agency as one of the conditions of probation. The security officer alerted security guards and discussed security precautions with the victim, ensuring there would be an effective response if the perpetrator violated this restriction.

7.17.4. Questions for the Agency Planning Group

1) Who at your agency would monitor the proceedings of the criminal case (e.g., to be aware of the situation if the perpetrator got out of jail on bail or probation)?
2) Does your security office maintain liaison with and keep in contact with agency or local law enforcement authorities in order to coordinate efforts in these types of cases?
3) Do you have a procedure in place for cleaning up the scene of the incident after investigators are finished examining it?
4) Would employees at your agency know who to call in an emergency (e.g., 911, FPS, in-house security, or in-house law enforcement)?

7.18. Case Study 16: Shooting

7.18.1. Incident

The report came in concerning the killing of two employees in the workplace and the wounding of two others. A witness had called 911 and the police and ambulances had arrived. The perpetrator, an agency employee, was taken into custody. The victims were sent to the hospital, and the police were interviewing witnesses and gathering evidence.

7.18.2. Response

In this situation, the agency's crisis response plan called for the immediate involvement of:

- A top management representative;
- A security officer;

- An employee relations specialist;
- An EAP counselor; and
- An official from the public affairs office.

Top Management Representative: was an assistant director of a field office with 800 employees. She coordinated the response effort as she was the senior person on duty at the time. In addition to acting as coordinator, she remained available to police throughout the afternoon to make sure there were no impediments to the investigation.

She immediately called the families of the wounded and assigned two other senior managers to notify the families of the deceased. She also arranged for a friend of each of the deceased coworkers to accompany each of the managers. She took care of numerous administrative details, such as authorizing expenditures for additional resources, signing forms, and making decisions about such matters as granting leave to co-workers. In this case, the police evacuated the building. Employees were told by the assistant director that they could go home for the rest of the day but were expected to return to duty the following day.

To ensure a coordinated response effort, she made sure agency personnel involved in the crisis had cell phones for internal communication while conducting their duties in various offices around the building.

Security Staff: assisted the police with numerous activities such as evacuating the building.

Employee Relations Specialist: contacted the agency's OGC and OIG and alerted them to the situation so they could immediately begin to monitor any criminal proceedings. The specialist made a detailed written record of the incident, but he did not take statements from witnesses as this could have impeded the criminal investigation and possible subsequent prosecution of the case. He also helped the supervisor draft a letter of proposed indefinite suspension of the perpetrator pending the outcome of the potential criminal matter. He worked closely with OGC, OIG, and the prosecutor's office to obtain relevant information as soon as it was available so the agency could proceed with administrative action when appropriate.

EAP Counselor: The agency had one EAP counselor on duty at the time. However, in prior planning for an emergency, the agency contracted with a local company to provide additional counselors on an "as needed" basis. The EAP counselor called the contractor, and four additional counselors were at the agency within an hour. The counselors remained available near the scene of the incident to reassure and comfort the employees. Since they were not agency employees, they wore readily visible identification badges.

After OIG received permission from the prosecutor's office, the agency EAP counselor arranged for a series of Critical Incident Stress Debriefings (CISDs) to take place two days later (see *Violence in the Federal Workplace: A Guide for Prevention and Response*, sections 5.5.2 and 5.7.3for a discussion of CISD). She also arranged for two contract EAP counselors to be at the workplace for the next week to walk around the offices inquiring how the employees were doing and to consult with supervisors about how to help the employees recover.

Public Affairs Officer: handled all aspects of press coverage. She maintained liaison with the media, provided an area for reporters to work, and maintained a schedule of frequent briefings. She worked closely with the agency's Office of Congressional Relations, who handled calls from congressional offices about the incident.

7.18.3. Resolution

When all of the employees in the office started using assertive statements, the abusive coworker became more cooperative. However, it took a written reprimand, a short suspension, and several counseling sessions with the EAP counselor before he ceased his shouting and rude behavior altogether.

7.18.4. Questions for the Agency Planning Group

1) How would your agency have obtained the services of additional EAP counselors?
2) How would employees be given information about this incident?
3) Who would clean up the crime scene?
4) Would you relocate employees who worked in the area of the crime scene?
5) What approach would your agency take regarding granting excused absence on the day of the incident and requests for leave in the days/ weeks following the incident?
6) How would you advise management to deal with work normally assigned to the victims/ perpetrator?
7) What support would your agency provide to supervisors to get the affected work group(s) back to functioning?

List of Abbreviations/Acronyms/Initializations

APA	American Psychiatric Association
BJAC	Bureau of Justice Assistance Clearinghouse
CISD	Critical Incident Stress Debriefings
CVE	Countering Violent Extremism
DBT	Design-Basis Threat
DHS	Department of Homeland Security
EAP	Employee Assistance Program
FAP	Federal Agency Programs
FBI	Federal Bureau of Investigations
FOUO	For Official Use Only
FPS	Federal Protective Service
FSL	Facility Security Level
HHS	Department of Health and Human Services
HR	Human Resource(s)
IACP	International Association of Chiefs of Police
ISC	Interagency Security Committee
LOP	Level of Protection
NCPC	National Crime Prevention Council
NIOSH	National Institute for Occupational Safety and Health
NOVA	National Organization for Victim Assistance
OGC	Office of General Counsel
OIG	Office of the Inspector General
OPM	Office of Personnel Management
OSHA	Occupational Safety and Health Administration
OWCP	Office of Workers Compensation Programs
PAVNET	Partnership Against Violence Network
USDA	United States Department of Agriculture
USSS	U.S. Secret Service

End Notes

[1] Executive Order No. 12977 (1995), "Interagency Security Committee."

[2] Interagency Security Committee, *Design-Basis Threat: An Interagency Security Committee Report (U),* 6th Ed., Washington D.C., 2012.

[3] Interagency Security Committee, (FOUO) *Facility Security Level Determinations for Federal Facilities: An Interagency Security Committee Standard*, Washington D.C.: Department of Homeland Security, 2008.

Index

A

B

G

H

I

J

K

L

M

N

O

R

S